TAKE a HIKE!

Family Walks
in the
Rochester Area

By Rich & Sue Freeman
Footprint Press
Fishers, New York

Edited by Diane Maggs
Cover by Image & Eye Graphics Services
Maps by Genesee/Finger Lakes Regional Planning Council

ISBN 0-9656974-6-0

Manufactured in the United States of America

Library of Congress Catalog Card Number: 97-90205

Locations by Trail Number

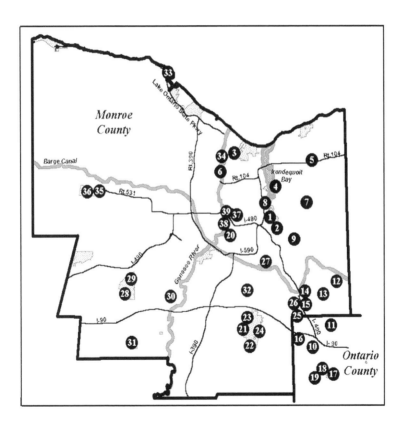

CONTENTS

Outdoor Walks Northeast of Rochester

 **Contents**

Contents

Outdoor Walks Southwest of Rochester

Outdoor Walks Northwest of Rochester

 **Contents**

Outdoor City Neighborhood Walks

Indoor Walks

Index

Acknowledgments

The research, writing, production, and promotion of a book such as this one is never a solitary adventure. "Take A Hike!" came into being because of the assistance of many wonderful people who freely shared their knowledge, experience, resources, thoughts, and time. We extend our heartfelt thanks to them all. Each in his or her own way is responsible for making the Rochester community a better place to live and, most of all, a community rich with the spirit of collaboration for the betterment of all. This is what ensures quality of life within a community. Thank you, each and every one.

American Heart Association

Joy Barnitz - Crescent Trail Association

Howard Beye - Finger Lakes Trail Conference

George Butt

Derek Doeffinger - Local Author

Rick French - Pack, Paddle, Ski Corporation

Fran Gotcsik - Friends of the Genesee Valley Greenway

John Green

Paul Howard - Genesee/Finger Lakes Regional Planning Council

Leigh Jones - Ganondagan State Historic Site

Eileen Kennedy - Mendon Ponds Park

Emerson Klees - Local Author

Diane Maggs - Editor

Skip Miller - Snow Country

Jeff Pingrey

Dave Rinaldo - Monroe County Parks Department

Amy Robinson - Image & Eye Graphics Services

Mary Anna Russo - Helmer Nature Center

8

Acknowledgements

Dave Schaeffer - Crescent Trail Association

Ron Sears

Shirley Shaw - Thousand Acre Swamp Sanctuary

Michelle Smith - Genesee/Finger Lakes Regional
    Planning Council

Dick Spade - Adirondack Mountain Club

Bill Starr

Bob Sundell

Cathy Towner - Genesee Transportation Council

Denny Tripp - Ellison Park

John Vaeth

Ron Walker - Hanson Nature Center

Dave Wright - Victor Hiking Trails, Inc.

Victor Yates - Pittsford Trails Coalition

Dave Zorn - Genesee/Finger Lakes Regional Planning Council

Introduction

Take a hike or a short walk. It's good for you. In as little as one hour you can do your body a favor - stretch your legs, raise your heart rate, and decrease your stress level. Hiking is a perfect exercise to balance today's hectic lifestyle.

Over the past years we have enjoyed hiking in many states throughout the United States. It didn't matter if it was a brief walk or extended backpacking trip. Every time we ventured outside, mother nature offered something new and wonderful. We learned it's not necessary to go far to reap these benefits. Rochester and the surrounding towns are a treasure trove of great walks. The geographic terrain varies greatly and wildlife is abundant. The state, city, and counties have had the vision to create parks and save wetlands, many with trails. Some are well known, while others are only known to the "locals." The hikes in this book are a few of our favorite ones, but there are so many more. In the back of this book is a listing of resources - organizations that are very helpful if you are interested in exploring more of what Monroe and the surrounding counties have to offer.

We thought we had hiked most of Rochester's trails, but we discovered many new ones just by talking with other hikers and local residents. At first they couldn't think of any trails, but soon they began to list interesting places that might have a hiking path. Even they were amazed at the number of trails they thought of. This created a wonderful list of potential adventures to keep on hand when the call of the outdoors came or we had just a few hours to spend. Our file grew to almost 200 tempting places to explore. This book focuses on short trails (under seven miles) within the immediate Rochester area. And, because we've lived here all our lives and know the full wrath of winter, we've included a few indoor walking options.

Many of these trails were built and are maintained by volunteer or community groups. They all welcome new members. We encourage everyone to join and benefit from the wide range of resources available in the Rochester community. All trails listed in this book are free and open to the public. You do not have to be a member of the sponsoring group to enjoy the trails.

If you find inaccurate information or substantially different conditions, please send a note detailing your findings to: Footprint Press, P.O. Box 645, Fishers, NY 14453.

How To Use This Book

We have clustered the hikes into six groups using downtown Rochester as the center dividing point:

Outdoor Walks Northeast of Rochester
Outdoor Walks Southeast of Rochester
Outdoor Walks Southwest of Rochester
Outdoor Walks Northwest of Rochester
Outdoor City Neighborhood Walks
Indoor Walks

We selected the trails with variety in mind. Some of the better known trails are popular and heavily traveled. Other, lesser known trails are secluded and lightly traveled. We also selected trails which are fairly easy to follow. Areas with many intersecting trails (where even we got lost) were excluded.

Where possible, we have designated hikes that go in a loop to let you see as much as possible without backtracking. You can easily begin and end in one location and not worry about finding transportation back to the beginning.

Approximate hiking times are given, but of course this depends on your speed. If you stop to watch the wildlife, enjoy the views, or read the descriptive plaques, it will take you longer than the time given. You'll notice that many of the hikes also have shortcuts or are connected to other trails that allow you to adjust your time.

Sketch maps for each trail are just that, sketches. We wanted maps that were easy to view and understand so everyone could be comfortable looking at where they would be going and what they would be seeing. Some of the sketches were taken from more detailed maps showing overall, general location relative to intersecting trails and landscape features. Some areas had never been mapped for hiking trails prior to this book.

Legend

At the beginning of each trail listing, you will find a map and a description with the following information:

Location: The road(s) that mark the access points for the trail.

Endpoints: The parking area and start/end points for the trail.

Hiking Time: Approximate time to hike at a comfortable pace including time to enjoy the views.

Length: The round-trip length of the hike in miles (unless noted as one-way).

Difficulty:

    (1 boot) easy hiking, generally level trail

    (2 boots) rolling hills, gradual grades on trail

    (3 boots) gentle climbing required to follow the trail

    (4 boots) some strenuous climbing required

Surface: The materials that make up the trail surface for the major portion of the hike.

Trail Markings: Markings used to designate the trails in this book vary widely. Some trails are not marked at all but can be followed by cleared or worn paths. This doesn't pose a problem for the hiker as long as there aren't many intersecting, unmarked paths. Other trails are well marked with either signs, blazes, or markers and sometimes a combination of all three. Blazing

13

is done by the official group that maintains the trail.

Signs - wooden or metal signs with instructions in words or pictures.

Blazes - painted markings on trees showing where the trail goes. Many blazes are rectangular and placed at eye level. Colors may be used to denote different trails. If a tree has twin blazes beside one another, you should proceed cautiously because the trail either turns or another trail intersects.

Markers - small plastic or metal geometric shapes (square, round, triangular) nailed to trees at eye level to show where the trail goes. They also may be colored to denote different trails.

Uses: Each trail has a series of icons depicting the activity or activities allowed on the trail. These include:

 Hiking   Snowmobiling

 Biking   Horseback Riding

 Fishing   X-country skiing

14

Park Size: This heading is only listed if the trail is located in a park and is the total park size designated in acres.

Contact: The address and phone number of the organization to contact if you would like additional information or if you have any questions not answered in this book.

Map Legend

——	Trail	●	Water Tower
●——	Recommended Trail	☐	Park Land
▬ ▬	Alternate Trail	▦	Wetland / Swamp
IIIIIII	Boardwalk	▦	Lake / Pond
)(	Bridge	P	Parking Lot
⊠	Trail Junction Label	══	Road
+	Vehicle Barrier	┼┼┼	Railroad
■	Building	▬	Waterway

Directions

In the directions we often tell you to turn left or right. To avoid confusion in some instances we have noted a compass direction in parentheses according to the following:

(N) = north
(S) = south
(E) = east
(W) = west

Some trails have "Y" or "T" junctions. A "Y" junction indicates one path that turns into two paths. The direction we give is either bear left or bear right. A "T" junction is one path that ends at another. The direction is turn left or turn right.

Guidelines

Any adventure in the outdoors can be inherently dangerous. It's important to watch where you are going and keep an eye on children. Some of these trails are on private property where permission is benevolently granted by the landowners. Please respect the landowners and their property. Follow all regulations posted on signs and stay on the trails. Our behavior today will determine how many of these wonderful trails remain for future generations to enjoy.

Follow "no-trace" ethics whenever you venture outdoors. "No-trace" ethics means that the only thing left behind as evidence of your passing is your footprints. Carry out all trash you carry in. Do not litter. In fact, carry a plastic bag with you and pick up any litter you happen upon along the way. The trails included in this book are intended for day hikes. Please, no camping or fires.

As the trails age and paths become worn, trail work groups sometimes reroute the trails. This helps control erosion and allows vegetation to return. It also means that if a sign or marker doesn't appear as it is described in the book, it's probably due to trail improvement.

Remember:

Take only pictures, leave only footprints.

Please do not pick anything.

Preparations and Safety

You can enhance your time in the outdoors by dressing properly and carrying appropriate equipment. Even for a short day hike, take a small backpack or fanny pack with the following gear:

camera	flashlight
binoculars	insect spray or lotion
compass	water bottle with water
rain gear	nature guidebook(s) of flowers, birds, etc.
snacks	plastic bag to pick up trash

Many of the trails can be muddy. It's best to wear lightweight hiking boots or at least sturdy sneakers.

Walking sticks have been around for centuries, but they are finding new life and new forms in recent years. These sticks can be anything from a branch picked up along the trail to a two-hundred-dollar pair of poles designed with built-in springs and hand-molded grips. Using a stick is a good idea, especially in hilly terrain. It can take the pressure off of your knees and help you balance when crossing bridges or logs.

Hiking with children is good exercise as well as an opportunity for learning. Use the time to teach children how to read a compass, identify flowers, trees, birds, and animal tracks. You'll find books on each of these subjects in the public library. A list of trails with educational signs or vegetation markers is included in the index at the back of this book.

Make it fun by taking a different type of gorp for each hike. Gorp is any combination of dried foods that you eat as a snack. Examples are:

1) peanuts, M&Ms, and raisins
2) chocolate morsels, nuts, and granola
3) dried banana chips, sunflower seeds, and carob chips

Get creative and mix any combination of chocolate, carob, dried fruits, nuts, oats, granolas, etc. The bulk food section at your local grocery store is a wealth of ideas. Other fun snacks are marshmallows, popcorn, peanuts in shells, graham crackers, and beef jerky.

When hiking with a child, tie a string on a whistle and have your child wear it as a necklace for safety. Instruct your child to blow the whistle only if he or she is lost.

A Word about Dogs

Hiking with dogs can be fun with their keen sense of smell and different perspective on the world. Many times they find things that we would have passed by unnoticed. They're inquisitive about everything and make excellent companions. But to ensure that your "hiking companion" enjoys the time outside, you must control your dog. Dogs are required to be leashed on most maintained public trails. The reasons are numerous, but the top ones are to protect dogs, to protect other hikers, and to ensure your pet doesn't chase wildlife. Good dog manners go a long way toward creating goodwill and improving tolerance to their presence.

Most of the trails listed in this book welcome dogs. The only trails which prohibit dogs are:

3   Helmer Nature Center Trails

7   Thousand Acre Swamp Trails

21   Birdsong and Quaker Pond Trails at Mendon Ponds Park

32   Hansen Nature Center Trails

33   Braddock Bay Raptor Research Trail

39   Rochester City Skyway

40   Malls and Schools

Seasons

Most people head into the great outdoors in summer. Temperatures are warm, the days are long, and plants and wildlife are plentiful. Summer is a great time to go hiking. But, don't neglect the other seasons. Each season offers a unique perspective, and makes hiking the same trail seem like a totally different adventure. In spring, a time of rebirth, you can watch the leaves unfurl and the spring flowers burst.

Become a leaf peeper in fall. Venture forth onto the trails and take in the colorful splendor of a beautiful fall day. Listen to the rustle of newly fallen leaves under your feet and inhale the unique smell of this glorious season.

And, finally, winter. It may be cold out, but the leaves are off the trees and the views will never be better. You can more fully appreciate the variety of this area's terrain if you wander out in winter. It is also the perfect time to watch for animal tracks in the snow and test your identification skills.

Northeast
Section

Ellison Park

Irondequoit Creek winds through this wooded, hilly park. The first trail takes you around the historic section of Ellison Park highlighting some of the remnants of the lost city of Tryon. The second trail takes you to a little used, remote area of the park.

The lost city of Tryon was the dream of one man, Salmon Tryon. In 1797 he found what he thought was the ideal location for his city. It had everything needed to prosper: waterpower, timberland, a strategic location on land and water routes, a good harbor, and an increasing population.

However, within a year Salmon needed cash and sold the land to his brother, John and his partners. They built a business complex consisting of a warehouse, five-story mercantile, distillery, factory for making ash, and a shipping dock with boats. The distillery and ashery were put into operation first. Clearing trees then burning them produced potash, which was in great demand as an early fertilizer. Sacks of grain were cooked down into liquor.

Within Ellison Park is Fort Schuyler. The existing fort was erected as a WPA (Work Projects Administration) project in 1938 to commemorate the original colonial trading post that stood in this vicinity in 1721- 75 years before Tryon was founded. However, the original Ft. Schuyler was abandoned after only one year because it became too difficult to keep it supplied from Albany.

Where did Tryon go? Its decline began with John Tryon's death in 1807. In the midst of trying to settle the estate, his executor also died. The stone warehouse and dock were in dire need of repairs. Money was scarce and the property as a whole was impossible to sell. So the distillery was dismantled and individual lots were sold.

In addition to these problems, the War of 1812 added to the decline of commerce on Lake Ontario. Construction of the Erie Canal was the final blow to Tryon. The canal bypassed Irondequoit Bay and provided a safer route without the need to worry about the storms and high winds on the lake.

Ownership changed several times over the years until the twentieth century when residential areas in the town of Brighton sprang up in place of the old farmsteads. Monroe County bought most of what had been Tryon from the Ellison family in 1927 for the creation of Ellison Park.

Note: Three-inch, four-color embroidered patches are available to commemorate your hike. Send $2.75 for each patch to: Troop 55, Covenant United Methodist Church, 1124 Culver Road, Rochester, NY 14609.

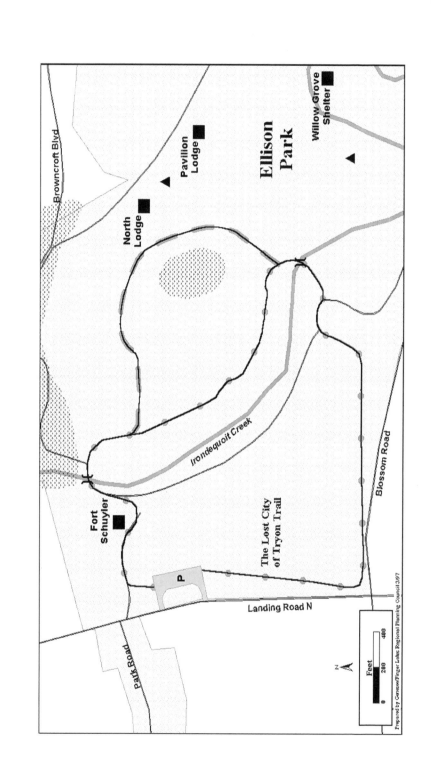

Willow Grove
Shelter

Ellison
Park

Pavilion
Lodge

Browncroft Blvd

North
Lodge

Irondequoit Creek

Fort
Schuyler

The Lost City
of Tryon Trail

Blossom Road

P

Landing Road N

Park Road

N

Feet

0   200   400

Prepared by Genesee/Finger Lakes Regional Planning Council 3/97

1.

Lost City of Tryon Trail

Location:	Ellison Park, Penfield (Landing Road N)
Endpoints:	parking lot on Landing Road N
Hiking Time:	45 minutes
Length:	1 mile
Difficulty:	👣 or 👣👣👣
Surface:	mowed grass path, paved road, gravel road
Trail Markings:	round orange plastic markers on trees on part of trail
Uses:	
Park Size:	447 acres
Contact:	Monroe County Parks Department
	171 Reservoir Avenue
	Rochester, NY 14620
	(716) 256-4950

Trail Directions

• From the parking lot, head right (S) uphill across the grass field toward the corner of Landing Road N. and Blossom Roads.

• Pass an old spring and cattail area on your right. If you look across the road you will see the "Old Tryon House" built in the late 1700s.

• Proceed to the corner of North Landing and Blossom Roads to the blue plaque in the corner rock in front of the Ellison Park sign.

27

- Head downhill, parallel to Blossom Road then bear left to the bottom of the hill.
- You'll pass a steep drop-off toward the left as you continue to bear left.
- Pass a small flight of stone steps on your left then turn right and take two flights of stone steps down to a paved road.
- Turn right and follow the road across a bridge over Irondequoit Creek.
- Now you have a choice. A short easy walk to the large rock or a steep climb around to the same large rock.

- EASY route -You may continue following the road as it bears left and follows the creek until you see a large rock on the left at the end of the mowed area.

- STEEP route -You may take the steep sandy hill on the right up to the crest of a ridge.
- Follow the ridge trail, bearing left at each junction. Keep the swampy pond far below to your left.
- After a steep descent, bear right and pass the Butler's Rangers plaque setting in the ground.
- Continue downhill until you reach an open field.
- Cross the field and a park road, heading toward the large rock.

BOTH trails meet here
- Facing the plaque in the rock, head to the right and cross the foot-bridge over Irondequoit Creek.
- Bear left, then after 50 yards turn right and head uphill. At the top of the hill is Fort Schuyler.
- Continue uphill until you meet a paved road. Follow the paved road to the right then take the gravel path off the left back to the parking lot.

"The mountains, rivers, earth, grasses, trees, and forests are always emanating a subtle, precious light, day and night, always emanating a subtle, precious sound, demonstrating and expounding to all people the unsurpassed ultimate truth."

Yuan-Sou

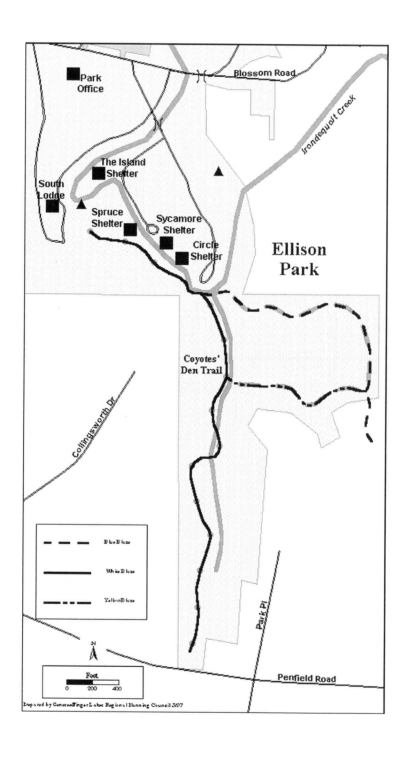

Park
Office

The Island
Shelter

South
Lodge

Spruce
Shelter

Sycamore
Shelter

Circle
Shelter

Ellison
Park

Irondequoit Creek

Blossom Road

Coyotes'
Den Trail

Collingsworth Dr.

Blue Blaze

White Blaze

Yellow Blaze

N

Feet
0   200   400

Park Pl

Penfield Road

Prepared by Genesee/Finger Lakes Regional Planning Council 2007

2.
Coyotes' Den Trail

Location:	Ellison Park, Penfield (off Blossom Road)
Endpoints:	South Lodge parking area
Hiking Time:	45 minutes
Length:	1 mile
Difficulty:	👞
Surface:	dirt path
Trail Markings:	white blazes on trees
Uses:	🚶
Park Size:	447 acres
Contact:	Monroe County Parks Department
	171 Reservoir Avenue
	Rochester, NY 14620
	(716) 256-4950

This trail leads back into an undeveloped area on the southern side of the park. After the first turn, you will feel surrounded by the closely formed hills. Coyotes inhabit the area and their tracks can sometimes be seen. Many large trees can be found in this area. One in particular is a White Oak listed in the National Registry of Big Trees. It's located at the end of the trail on the west side.

Trail Directions
• From the South Lodge parking area walk southeast toward the young hemlock (evergreen) trees.

Coyotes' Den Trail

- White blazes lead you along Irondequoit Creek. Turn right at a small creek. Watch for eastern coyote, red fox, and deer.
- Continue following the white blazes to the grassy opening on Penfield Road. Don't miss looking at the large White Oak tree to your right.
- Your return trip can be simply retracing your steps or you may choose to take a very steep yellow-blazed side trail.
- The steep yellow-blazed side trail is found half way back as you return on the white-blazed trail.
- The yellow blazes end at a "T." Turn left.(Trail to the right goes to the private Dolomite Products Co. property.)
- Trail brings you back to Irondequoit Creek near where you first began.

Helmer Nature Center

The Helmer Nature Center began operations in 1973 under the West Irondequoit School District. The center utilizes the natural world as a classroom, providing learning opportunities, encouraging environmental awareness, and fostering the concept of global stewardship. They offer a wide range of educational activities including nature awareness, animal habitats, snowshoeing, Native American culture, pioneer living, outdoor cooking, field studies, etc. This area was formerly comprised of vineyards with terracing which can still be seen across the wooded hills. After enjoying their trails, stop in the center to find out about the educational activities and consider becoming a member.

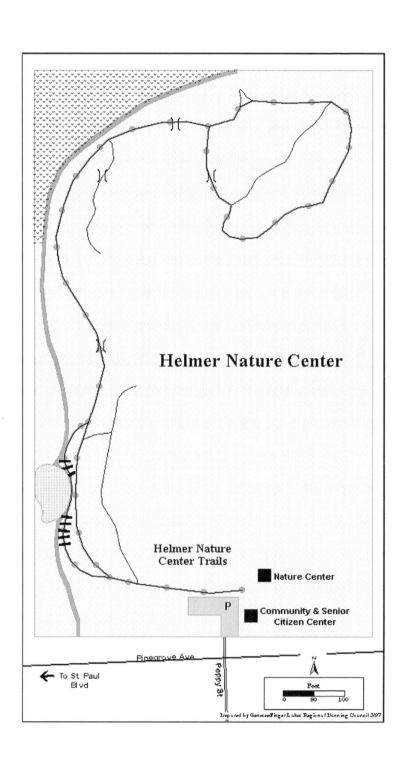

Helmer Nature Center

Helmer Nature
Center Trails

■ Nature Center

■ Community & Senior
Citizen Center

P

Pinegrove Ave

Poppy St

← To St Paul
Bl vd

N

Feet
0   50   100

Prepared by Genesee/Finger Lake Regional Planning Council 3/97

3.
Helmer Nature Center Trails

Location:	Pinegrove Avenue, Irondequoit (off St. Paul Boulevard)
Endpoints:	Nature Center parking lot
Hiking Time:	25 minutes
Length:	1 mile
Difficulty:	👣 👣
Surface:	wood chip path
Trail Markings:	overhead signs
Uses:	(pets are not allowed)
Park Size:	45 acres
Contact:	Helmer Nature Center
	154 Pinegrove Avenue
	Rochester, NY 14617
	(716) 336-3035

Trail Directions
· Begin on the Woodchuck Trail which takes you past a small pond, stream, and marsh area.
· Follow until the Woodchuck Trail ends and is met by the Eco Trail.
· Continue past a trail on the right to a four-way intersection.
· Go straight (Wolf Tree Trail) and follow around to the open field.
· Reenter the woods on the right and take the first left (Sugarbush Trail) to the end.
· Turn left again always taking the trail to the left back to the start.

Irondequoit Bay Park East

This county park is undeveloped and unknown even to most area residents. The trail goes to the bay's edge and offers a rugged hike back into steep, wooded ridges and valleys. There are many large hemlock and oak trees. If you decide to follow any one of the many side trails, be careful not to lose your way. Soon each valley and trail begins to look the same, adding another challenge to the hike!

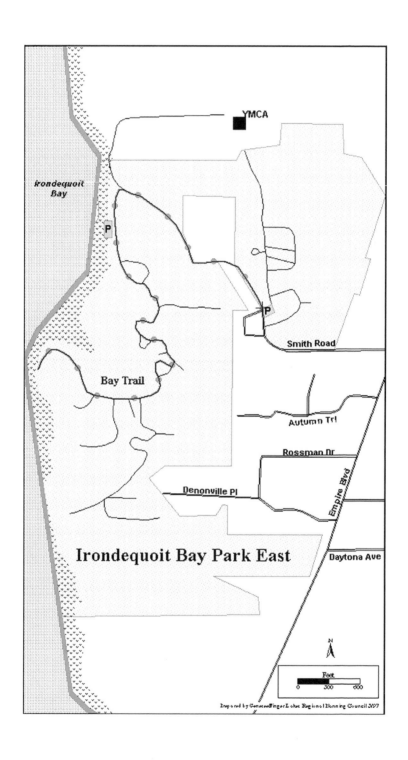

YMCA

Irondequoit
Bay

P

P

Smith Road

Bay Trail

Autumn Trl

Rossman Dr

Empire Blvd

Denonville Pl

Irondequoit Bay Park East

Daytona Ave

N

Feet

0   300   600

Prepared by Genesee/Finger Lakes Regional Planning Council 2007

4.
Bay Trail

Location:	Smith Road, Penfield (off Empire Boulevard)
Endpoints:	grass parking area beside circle at the end of Smith Road
Hiking Time:	1 hour
Length:	2 miles
Difficulty:	👣 👣 👣 👣
Surface:	gravel path, dirt path
Trail Markings:	white blazes
Uses:	
Park Size:	182 acres
Contact:	Monroe County Parks Department
	171 Reservoir Avenue
	Rochester, NY 14620
	(716) 256-4950

Trail Directions

· From the circle follow the road down the hill (W) past a Town of Penfield building.

· At the bottom of the hill, turn left. (Trail to the right goes to the Bay View YMCA.)

· Pass a metal building used by the YMCA in the summer and follow the white blazes on the trees.

· Climb a hill skirting the left side.

· Trail turns right and proceeds downhill.

· At the bottom turn left crossing a small stream.
· Trail ascends hill.
· At the "Y" bear right away from the creek, followed quickly by another right turn.
· Continue following the blazes along the ridge of a hill.
· Trail descends to a peninsula at the bay's edge.
· To return follow the blazes back to the gravel road.

Bonus:

Behind the parking area are more trails that cover a small area on level ground. The main trail leads to the Bay View YMCA, while another goes over to the lilac nursery for the Monroe County Department of Parks.

North Ponds Park

North Ponds is known for its summer swimming area. It has a level trail which circumnavigates the park's two largest ponds and makes a nice stroll at any time of the year. The area can be somewhat noisy from traffic on nearby Route 104. (Pay parking for the swimming area is located on the westbound Route 104 access road).

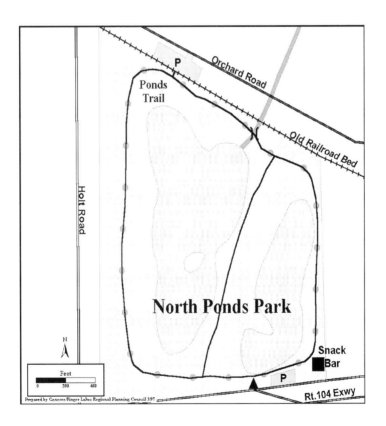

41

5.
Ponds Trail

Location: North Ponds Park, Webster (off Orchard Street)

Endpoints: Parking lot on Orchard Street is free. Parking lot at the westbound Route 104 entrance ramp off North Avenue is a pay lot during summer months.

Hiking Time: 25 minutes

Length: 1.3 miles

Difficulty:

Surface: gravel path and paved path

Trail Markings: none

Uses:

Park Size: 55 acres

Contact: Webster Parks, Recreation and Community Services
1000 Ridge Road
Webster, NY 14580
(716) 872-2911

Trail Directions

· From the parking lot on Orchard Street, follow the path into the park.
· At the "Y" junction bear right.
· Follow the path, bearing left as it winds around the ponds, past the restrooms, swimming area, snack bar, etc.
· Bear right at the "Y" junction. (Left path leads between the two ponds to a picnic area.)
· Turn right at the next junction to return to the parking lot.

42

Seneca Park

This park was designed by Frederick Law Olmsted who is considered to be the founder of landscape architecture. He was prolific in the Rochester area where he designed four major parks: Seneca, Genesee Valley, Highland, and Maplewood.

Olmsted's designs were revolutionary for the late 1800s. Instead of laying out precise squares and gardens, he planned clumps of woods, meandering trails, bridle paths and spectacular views. He planted trees carefully to effect a "forested" look. This natural, quiet look was half of Olmsted's design philosophy. The other half was the creation of spaces for more active use, such as the open areas for baseball fields and ponds for swimming in summer and ice skating in winter. Pavilions and bridges designed in a neo-classic style separate activity areas.

Within Seneca Park is Trout Lake. In its days of grandeur, swan boats plied back and forth taking passengers for a ride. Fifteen to 20 passengers rode on bench seats while the driver perched on a cast iron seat between two 4 foot high swans and peddled the pontoon boat.

Seneca Park and the trail run adjacent to the steep Genesee River gorge. Along the trail are four dock access trails leading to the river's edge. Hiking down reveals the 400 million years of geologic history in the gorge walls. On the trail you pass wetlands, a pond, and many beautiful scenic views of the river. The park is also home to the Seneca Park Zoo.

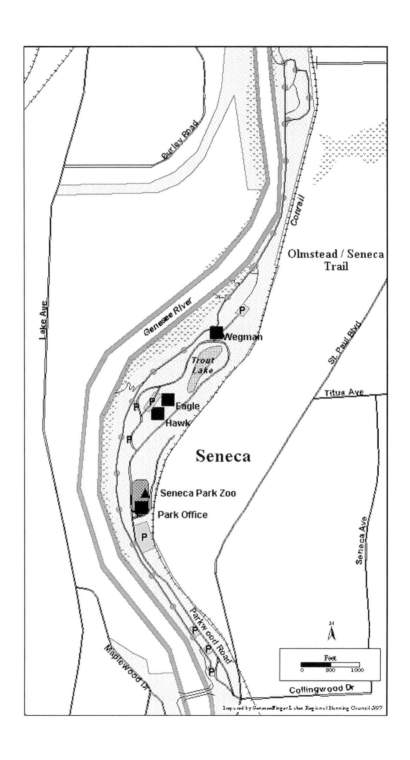

Burley Road

Lake Ave

Genesee River

Contrail

Olmstead / Seneca
Trail

P

Wegman

Trout
Lake

St. Paul Blvd.

Titus Ave.

P
P Eagle

Hawk

P

Seneca

P

Seneca Park Zoo

Park Office

Seneca Ave.

P

N

Parkwood Road

P

P

Feet
0   500   1000

Maplewood Dr.

P

Collingwood Dr.

Prepared by Genesee/Finger Lakes Regional Planning Council 2007

6.
Olmsted/Seneca Trail

Location:	entrance to Seneca Park Zoo, Rochester (off St. Paul Boulevard)
Endpoints:	first car turnaround after entering park
Hiking Time:	2.5 hours
Length:	4.2 miles
Difficulty:	👣 👣 👣
Surface:	woodchip path, gravel path
Trail Markings:	none
Uses:	🚶
Park Size:	297 acres
Contact:	Monroe County Parks Department
	171 Reservoir Avenue
	Rochester, NY 14620
	(716) 256-4950

Trail Directions

· Begin at the first turnaround circle as you enter the park near the Monroe County Pure Waters bridge built in 1988. The 670-foot pedestrian bridge gives an excellent view of the surrounding gorge and river 100 feet below. The trail runs parallel to the park road entrance. The road provides additional areas to park and pick up the trail. While there are no blazes, the trail is well defined and up to eight feet wide at times.

· After passing the zoo parking lot, follow the trail down to the fence opening on the left which was made to allow hikers only, and skinny ones at that, to pass through.

45

· Begin an easy descent on a wood chip path. Because the trail is in a park, there are many side trails off to the right. Stay on the main trail always heading north, staying near the river gorge.

· Pass your first lookout. This is a nice place to sit on the bench and enjoy the view.

· Cross a small bridge over a stream and follow around to the left.

· Proceed gradually downward over two wooden walkways.

· Trail off to the left goes down to a dock on the Genesee River. This is the first of four dock trails you'll have the chance to take, if you want to.

· Pass additional views with benches.

· Cross a wooden bridge over a small creek.

· At the fork bear right. Trail to left is the second dock trail to the river. The third dock trail on the left soon follows. This is called Olmsted Landing after Frederick Law Olmsted, the park's designer.

· Trail now meets a gravel park access road. Follow the road, continuing to head north through a 10-foot high fence gate.

· This is the narrowest part of the park with the gorge on the left and a railroad and private homes on the right.

· Pass a gated access road on the right used by the park for composting.

· Turn right at the small marked side trail.

· Turn right again and pass the locked Seneca Road entrance (locked to vehicles, open to pedestrians).

· Follow trail around to the left leading back to the gorge.

· Next you will come to a four-way intersection. This is the farthest point north for the trail. One of the two trails on the right leads to the river, while the other continues heading north to the end of county property and a locked gate. Bear left and begin your return trip heading south along the gorge.

· Emerge back on the gravel access road.

· Turn right (S) and follow the access road until you pass the open fence gate.

· Immediately watch for a trail on the right.

· At this point you will be retracing your steps back to where you began. Remember to stay on the trail nearest the gorge.

Thousand Acre Swamp

White trilliums, ferns, and blue violets are among the 500 plant species known to inhabit the Thousand Acre Swamp Sanctuary, along with large hardwood species of northern red oak, white oak, sugar maple, and black cherry. They share the land with deer, rabbit, red and grey fox, muskrat, opossum, mink, eastern coyote, and over 147 species of birds. It's no wonder that the Central and Western New York Chapter of the Nature Conservancy chose these lands for preservation.

The Thousand Acre Swamp Sanctuary is a great place to watch marsh life up close. It's easy to spot animal footprints in the mud and get an up-close look at frogs, snapping turtles, and geese nesting. Bring binoculars for the best viewing. Local legend has it that the sanctuary was once the home of a gentleman who wanted to "get away from the world."

Trails can be muddy and in warm weather, bring along your insect repellent. Guided hikes, offered on weekends from April through the end of October, cover a wide variety of interesting subjects such as wildflowers, coyotes, hidden worlds, and photography. Contact the Nature Conservancy for the latest schedule.

The Nature Conservancy is a non-profit international membership organization committed to global preservation of natural diversity. The Central and Western New York Chapter has protected more than 13,000 acres and owns and manages 29 nature sanctuaries in this region.

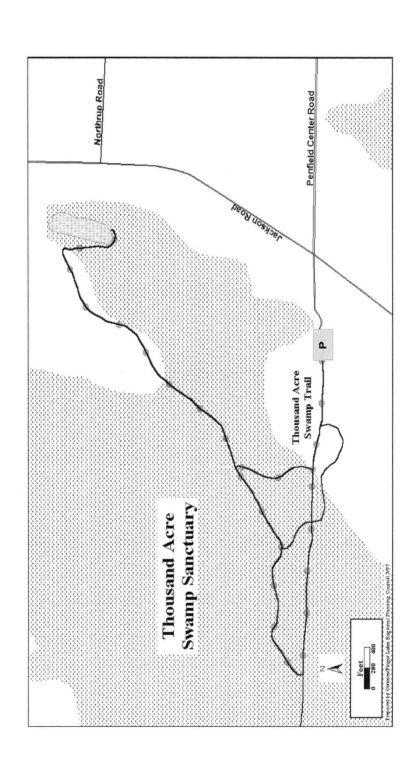

Thousand Acre Swamp Sanctuary

Thousand Acre Swamp Trail

Northrup Road

Jackson Road

Penfield Center Road

P

N

Feet
0   200   400

Prepared by Genesee/Finger Lakes Regional Planning Council 3/97

7.
Thousand Acre Swamp Trail

Location:	Jackson Road, Penfield (between Atlantic Avenue and Plank Road)
Endpoints:	sanctuary parking area just north of Penfield Volunteer Ambulance
Hiking Time:	1.5 hours
Length:	2.6 miles
Difficulty:	
Surface:	dirt path and boardwalks
Trail Markings:	signs
Uses:	(pets are not allowed)
Park Size:	650 acres
Contact:	The Nature Conservancy
	315 Alexander Street
	Rochester, NY 14604
	(716) 546-8030

49

Trail Directions

· From the parking lot, head west on the entrance trail.

· Pass the junctions of Song Bird Trail, Trillium Trail, and Weasel Way.

· Turn right on Boardwalk.

· Turn left on Warbler Fen.

· Bear left on Hermit Walk.

· Hermit Walk turns into The Meadows which turns into The Way Pond Trail.

· The Way Pond Trail skirts the south end of Way Pond and then dead-ends.

· Turn around and walk back along The Way Pond Trail, The Meadows, and Hermit Walk.

· Turn left at Trillium Trail.

· Turn left at Deer Run and follow the entrance trail back to the parking lot.

Tryon Park

Tyron Park, dedicated in 1971, is a hilly wooded oasis within a populated city area. It's a delightful walk through mature woods with views of Irondequoit Bay. The noise of Interstate 590 reminds you that civilization isn't far away. The park is on the site of the city's old sewage plant, but all that remains is an above-ground delivery pipe.

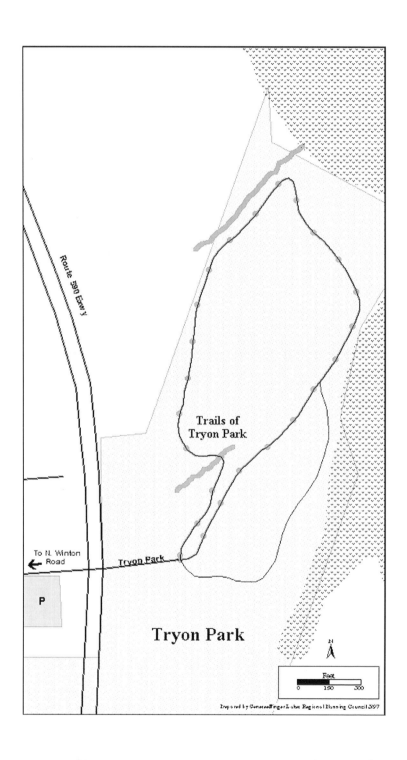

Route 590 Exw'y

Trails of
Tryon Park

To N. Winton
← Road

Tryon Park

P

Tryon Park

N

Feet
0   150   300

Prepared by Genesee/Finger Lakes Regional Planning Council 2007

8.
Tryon Park Trail

Location:	Tryon Park Road, Rochester (off North Winton Road)
Endpoints:	park on Tryon Park Road before Interstate 590 overpass or at the end of Loudisa Drive in the baseball field parking area. Do not park between Interstate 590 and the trailhead.
Hiking Time:	45 minutes
Length:	1.1 miles
Difficulty:	👣 👣
Surface:	wooded path
Trail Markings:	white blazes on trees
Uses:	🚶
Park Size:	80 acres, undeveloped
Contact:	Monroe County Parks Department
	171 Reservoir Avenue
	Rochester, NY 14620
	(716) 256-4950

Trees and shrubs are numbered along the trail with three-inch round orange disks. Watch for the numbers and test your tree identification skills.

1. Northern Red Oak
2. Sugar Maple
3. Tulip Tree
4. White Oak
5. Basswood
6. Flowering Dogwood
7. Sassafras
8. White Pine
9. Red Osier Dogwood
10. Buckthorn
11. Cottonwood
12. Pignut Hickory
13. Gray Birch
14. Black Locust
15. Ailanthus
16. Box Elder
17. Black Oak
18. Shadbush
19. Cherry
20. Blue Beech (Ironwood)
21. Hop Hornbeam
22. American Beech
23. Black Cherry
24. Black Birch
25. Canadian Hemlock

Trail Directions
· At end of Tyron Park Road, bear left on the old abandoned road. (A separate trail heads right over a manhole cover.) You'll pass under the old sewage delivery pipe.
· Carefully follow the white blazes on the trees. There are many intersecting, unblazed trails.
· The trail leads to a view of the Irondequoit Creek wetlands area with Irondequoit Bay to the north.
· Continue following the white blazes back to Tryon Park Road.

Linear Park

This area of Irondequoit Creek is known as "The Falls" because the creek drops 90 feet in one mile. At one time many mills lined the creek and, if you look closely, you'll see some foundations that still remain. In the fall this is also a good place to watch salmon going upstream to spawn. This is a "linear" trail which means you will be returning on the same trail.

9.
The Falls Trail

Location:	Linear Park, Penfield (off Route 441)
Endpoints:	parking lot at end of Linear Park Drive
Hiking Time:	45 minutes
Length:	1.5 miles
Difficulty:	
Surface:	dirt path
Trail Markings:	none
Uses:	
Contact:	Town of Penfield
	3100 Atlantic Avenue
	Penfield, NY 14526
	(716) 377-8674

Trail Directions

· Begin at the "Trail" sign and walk upstream (E).

· Continue following the stream on your left and cross four bridges that span small ravines.

· Trail crosses small side stream; continue straight.

· Trail slowly narrows and finally ends.

· Retrace your steps to the parking area.

Southeast
Section

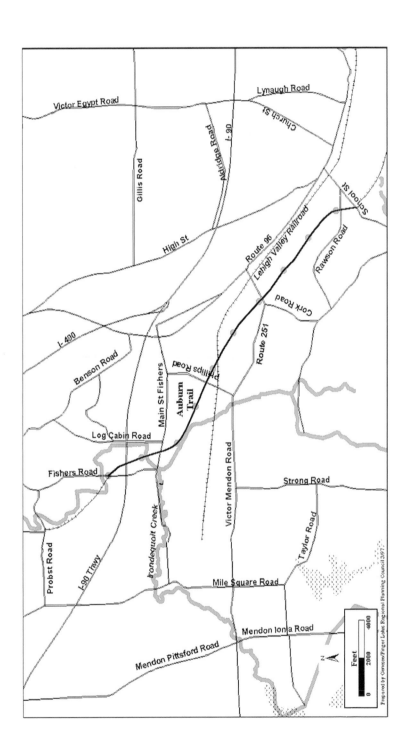

10.
Auburn Trail

Location:	Fishers and Victor, NY
Endpoints:	Fishers Road and School Street, Victor
Hiking Time:	5 hours (round trip)
Length:	7.8 miles (round trip)
Difficulty:	
Surface:	cinder path, mowed grass path, some ballast stone
Trail Markings:	3.5-inch white, rectangular, metal, Victor Hiking Trail markers and 11-inch green and yellow Victor Hiking Trail signs
Uses:	
Contact:	Victor Hiking Trails, Inc.
	85 East Main Street
	Victor, NY 14564

Auburn Trail

This is a linear rather than a loop trail. You can do the whole trail by parking a car at either end or pick any segment and go out and back. Park along the roadway at any trail crossing or in back of the Fishers Firehouse on Main Street, Fishers.

The Auburn Trail was one of the first trails opened by Victor Hiking Trails. This volunteer group was conceived by the Victor Conservation Board in the 1980s. The first organizational meeting occurred in September 1991 and the Auburn Trail opened in September 1993. Victor Hiking Trails offers monthly guided hikes in the Rochester area and welcomes new members.

The Auburn Trail was once the bustling Rochester and Auburn Railroad. No rails or ties remain on the railroad bed; they have been gone for years. The trail is grass, cinder, and loose stone in some areas. And, yes, it is flat which makes for very pleasant walking. In fact, you are in for many surprises as you walk its length.

You will pass through a spectacular tunnel under the New York State Thruway. The tunnel was built large enough for trains to pass through. At another point, two former railroads cross so you will walk under an old railroad trestle which was used by the Lehigh Valley Railroad.

Nature is plentiful along the way. Part of the rail bed is raised to overlook beautiful swamp and pond areas. Look carefully along the way and you may be able to pick some blackberries for a quick snack. The trail abounds with birds, beaver, deer, and muskrats. From their pens along the way, geese may honk at you or a bull may give you the eye.

History will also surround you. Be sure to watch for the old potato storage building and old rail sidings as you pass through Fishers. Stop to admire the 1845 cobblestone railroad pump house (adjacent to the Fishers firehouse). It's the oldest railroad building left in the country. Concrete "tombstones" along the way were mile-posts for the trains. One marked "S 85" denoted that Syracuse was

85 miles away. A "W" in the concrete marker told the engineer a road crossing was coming and to blow the train's whistle. See if you can find a rectangular concrete box partly buried in the ballast. This battery box was used to power the signals at road crossings if the main power was down.

Trail Directions
· Fishers Road to Main Street, Fishers	0.6 mile
· Main Street, Fishers to Phillips Road	0.9 mile
· Phillips Road to Route 251	1.1 miles
· Route 251 to Rawson Road	1.1 miles
· Rawson Road to School Street	0.2 miles

"We cannot remember too often that when we observe nature, and especially the ordering of nature, it is always ourselves alone we are observing."

G. C. Lichtenberg (1742-99)
German physicist, philosopher

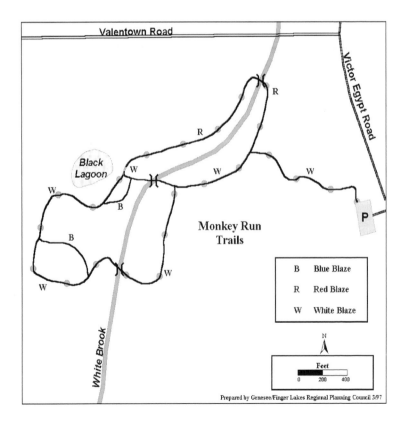

11.
Monkey Run Trails

Location:	Victor-Egypt Road, Victor (near the corner of Valentown Road)
Endpoints:	gravel parking lot in a field on right side of Victor-Egypt Road (can be difficult to locate)
Hiking Time:	40 minutes
Length:	1.3 miles
Difficulty:	
Surface:	dirt path and mowed grass path
Trail Markings:	3.5-inch white, red, and blue, rectangular, metal, Victor Hiking Trail markers and 11-inch green and yellow Victor Hiking Trail signs
Uses:	
Contact:	Victor Hiking Trails, Inc.
	85 East Main Street
	Victor, NY 14564

The present day Valentown Road was formerly known as Monkey Run. The winding road reminded residents of a jungle vine wrapping around one tree after another possibly providing a means of transport for an imaginary troop of monkeys.

Monkey Run Trails are entirely on private property. Please follow posted signs and respect the rights of the landowners who are allowing you to experience their secluded haven.

This is a pleasant walk in the woods dotted with numerous types of beautiful wildflowers in the spring- bring your nature guide book. And if you're lucky you'll see the snapping turtles in the "Black Lagoon."

Trail Directions
· The trail leaves from the north corner of the parking lot.
· Follow the white markers.
· Turn right at the red trail junction.
· Cross White Brook and follow the culvert between White Brook and the hill.
· Turn right on the white trail and pass the "Black Lagoon."
· The trail leads along a farmers field, then back into the woods.
· Cross White Brook heading uphill to the "T" junction.
· Turn right (E) and follow the white trail back to the parking lot.

Trail Town USA

In 1996, Perinton was named one of the top 10 "Trail Towns" in the United States by the American Hiking Association. The association recognizes communities that use trails to provide exercise for the body, stimulation of the mind and senses, and a personal connection with the community's natural beauty and past history. The forty miles of trails including Crescent Trail, Erie Canal Heritage Trail, and the Perinton Hike-Bike Way achieve this goal within Perinton.

The Crescent Trail Association

A FOOTPATH IN PERINTON

The Crescent Trail Association is a volunteer organization which was organized in 1980 to develop, promote, and maintain public hiking trails in the Town of Perinton. Currently, they have over 27 miles of trails passing through woods, marshland, and meadows. The trails converge into the Erie Canal Heritage Trail and an old trolley-bed trail, The Perinton Hike-Bike Way.

Many individual landowners have granted permission for trails to cross their property. The continued use of the trails and the opening of additional sections depend upon hikers respecting the rights of landowners.

-Stay on the trail   -Leave no rubbish
-Protect trees and crops   -Use no motorized vehicles
-Start no fires   -Ride no bicycles

The Crescent Trail Association welcomes new members. They sponsor a guided hike along a portion of their trails on the second Sunday of each month. Hikes are open to the public.

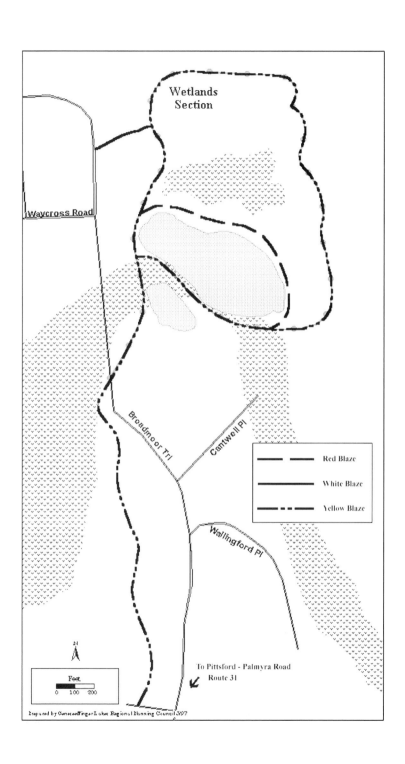

Wetlands
Section

Waycross Road

Broadmoor Trl

Cantwell Pl

Red Blaze

White Blaze

Yellow Blaze

Wallingford Pl

N

To Pittsford - Palmyra Road
Route 31

Feet

0   100   200

Prepared by Genesee/Finger Lakes Regional Planning Council 2007

12.
Wetlands Section

Location:	Broadmoor Trail Road, Perinton (off Route 31)
Endpoints:	Broadmoor Trail Road (park along the edge of the road where a small stream passes under)
Hiking Time:	20 minutes
Length:	0.8 mile
Difficulty:	
Surface:	mowed grass path and dirt path
Trail Markings:	3-inch Crescent Trail logo with trail color indicated in the bottom portion
Uses:	
Contact:	The Crescent Trail Association
	P.O. Box 1354
	Fairport, NY 14450

A wonderful, easy stroll through fields and woods, this trail passes near streams and ponds with active beaver. You may notice trees the beaver have eaten, two beaver dens, and many beaver trails.

Trail Directions
· Head northeast along the stream following the Crescent Trail sign (yellow trail).
· Pass the first pond on the right. (Houses will be on your left.)
· At the junction turn right and follow the yellow trail.
· At the next junction turn right onto the blue trail and cross a wooden bridge.
· Cross three more bridges.
· At the next junction go left to stay on the blue trail.
· Continue straight, past the intersecting red trail and passing along the part of the yellow trail you've already been on, to the parking area at Broadmoor Trail Road.

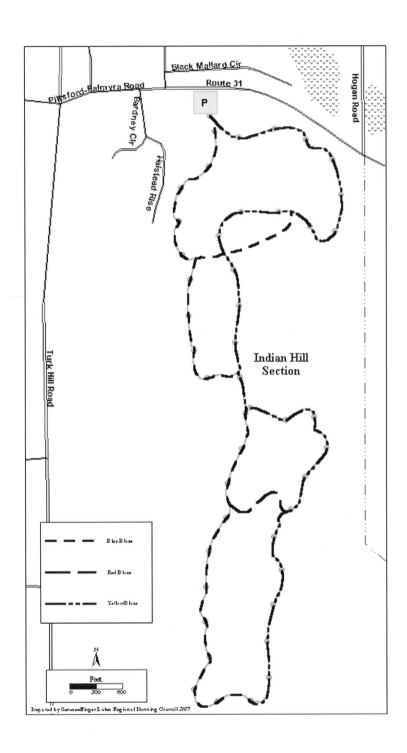

Black Mallard Cir

Route 31

Pittsford-Palmyra Road

Hogan Road

Eardney Cir

Halstead Rise

P

Indian Hill
Section

Turk Hill Road

Blue Blaze

Red Blaze

Yellow Blaze

N

Feet
0   300   600

Prepared by Genesee/Finger Lakes Regional Planning Council 2007

13.
Indian Hill Section

Location:	Route 31, Perinton (east of Route 250)
Endpoints:	parking lot on Route 31 between Turkhill Road and the hamlet of Egypt
Hiking Time:	1 hour
Length:	2.1 miles
Difficulty:	🐾 🐾 🐾
Surface:	dirt path
Trail Markings:	blazes painted on trees and small square colored markers
Uses:	🚶
Contact:	The Crescent Trail Association P.O. Box 1354 Fairport, NY 14450

Well-blazed and easy-to-follow, this trail goes through meadows and woods to a high vantage point (elevation 714 feet) overlooking suburban Perinton and the Rochester skyline in the distance.

Trail Directions

· From the parking lot, head straight uphill. (Follow blue blazes out-bound and yellow blazes for the return.)
· Stay on the blue-blazed trail as you pass several intersecting trails.
· At the field turn right and continue on the blue trail into a narrow woods.
· At the next junction turn left and head downhill along the edge of a field.
· At a junction turn right on the yellow trail for a short distance.
· At the next junction go right on the blue trail again. Pass the red trail.
· Cross over a dirt farm road and head past a pond on your left.
· Follow the blue trail as it bends left.
· As you emerge into a mowed field, watch for a sign saying "Stop - end of Crescent Trail." Turn left onto the yellow trail and walk along the edge of a field.
· At the far corner of the field, turn right and take a sharp left into the woods. Head downhill.
· Watch for the trail to turn right after a plank bridge. (The red trail goes straight.)
· The trail turns left and crosses another plank bridge.
· Follow the yellow blazes as the trail twists. Climb a steep hill.
· At the junction with the blue trail, turn right and stay on yellow.
· At the second junction with blue, again bear right and stay on yellow.
· Follow the edge of a field as you head uphill.
· Carefully follow the yellow blazes. (The trail will turn left but you could easily make a mistake and continue straight.)
· Emerge into a field and the top of the hill. Be sure to pause and enjoy the view.
· Choose the middle trail to stay on yellow.
· Again, follow the yellow blazes carefully; you'll pass intersecting trails.
· At the intersection with the blue trail, continue straight, staying on yellow.
· The trail bends sharply left.
· The trail now runs parallel to Route 31 as it takes you back to the parking lot.

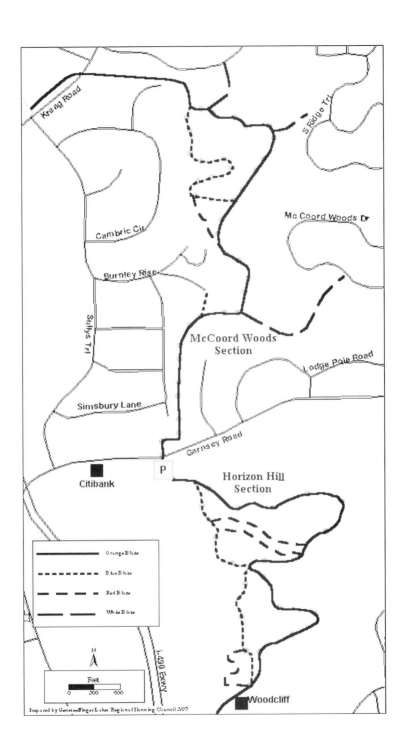

Kreag Road

S Ridge Trl

Mc Coord Woods Dr

Cambric Cir

Burnley Rise

Sullys Trl

McCoord Woods
Section

Lodge Pole Road

Simsbury Lane

Garnsey Road

P

Citibank

Horizon Hill
Section

Orange Blaze
Blue Blaze
Red Blaze
White Blaze

N

Feet
0   300   600

I-490 Expwy

Woodcliff

Prepared by Genesee/Finger Lakes Regional Planning Council 2007

14.
McCoord Woods Section

Location:	Garnsey Road, Perinton (Interstate 490, exit Bushnell's Basin, left Route 96 (S), left on Garnsey Road)
Endpoints:	parking lot on Garnsey Road
Hiking Time:	75 minutes
Length:	2.3 miles
Difficulty:	👣 👣 👣 👣
Surface:	dirt path
Trail Markings:	blazes painted on trees
Uses:	🚶
Contact:	The Crescent Trail Association
	P.O. Box 1354
	Fairport, NY 14450

This well-blazed, easy-to-follow trail begins as a narrow stretch of land between the backyards of private homes but quickly turns to wilderness in terrain sculpted by glaciers. For a quick escape from civilization, this trail can't be beat.

McCoord Woods Section

Trail Directions

· From the parking lot, cross Garnsey Road and head north on the trail at the Crescent Trail sign with an orange marker.

· Bear right to cross a bridge over a small creek.

· Follow the orange blazes through backyards where the trail turns left and enters the woods.

· As you hike along, a small creek is on your left.

· Continue on the orange trail (white blaze trail enters from right) and cross a bridge.

· Several small trails lead off, stay on the orange trail.

· Follow switchbacks up a steep hillside.

· Bear right on the orange trail as it intersects the red trail.

· The trail heads uphill to the top of an esker. (Sorry, no view.)

· Stay on the orange trail as you pass another white trail.

· At the blue trail junction leave orange and take a left (S) on the blue trail.

· Cross a plank bridge.

· At the orange trail junction turn right onto the orange trail.

· Follow the orange trail back to the parking lot.

13.

Horizon Hill Section

A FOOTPATH IN PERINTON

Location:	Garnsey Road, Perinton (Interstate 490, exit Bushnell's Basin, left on Route 96 (S), left on Garnsey Road)
Endpoints:	parking lot on Garnsey Road
Hiking Time:	1 hour
Length:	2.3 miles
Difficulty:	
Surface:	dirt path
Trail Markings:	blazes painted on trees and small plastic markers
Uses:	
Contact:	The Crescent Trail Association
	P.O. Box 1354
	Fairport, NY 14450

Hilly terrain on this hike makes it great for a short, strenuous workout. The trail wanders through the hills in the woods between Garnsey Road and Woodcliff Lodge giving a spectacular view of the Irondequoit Creek Valley and Rochester in the distance. There are many intersecting trails but the main trails are very well marked with blazes and markers. Watch carefully for double blazes which signal trail intersections or turns. The loop described here follows the orange trail outbound and the blue trail returning.

You may want to use this trail to test your child's blaze-following abilities. Or, as a treat for yourself or your family, hike to Woodcliff Lodge for brunch, then hike back.

Trail Directions

· From the parking lot head east on the orange trail.
· Continue straight on the orange trail as it crosses a bridge and heads uphill. (The blue trail goes to the right.)
· Cross two more small bridges.
· Watch for the double orange blazes at the top of a climb; the orange trail turns right.
· Cross a short boardwalk. Then at "Allan's Walk" sign, turn left and cross the bridge. (Straight takes you to the red trail.)
· Climb a hill. Turn right at the double blaze and you'll emerge into a clearing with a view of downtown Rochester. There's a bench to sit and savor the view.
· Pass the bench, turn left, and continue on the orange trail.
· Bear left and stay on the orange trail as you climb another hill. (The blue trail heads off to the right.)
· Watch for double blazes and turn right half way up a hill.
· Descend, then ascend again. Toward the top of the hill watch for double blazes and turn right. (Straight goes to the Woodcliff golf course fairway.)
· The trail bears right just before the Woodcliff grounds-keeping equipment and diesel tanks.
· Turn left at the double blazes.
· Bear right at the next double blazes. (Left goes to Woodcliff Lodge.)
· Shortly, watch for the blue blazes on the right. Turn right and begin the return leg on the blue trail. (Or you can continue on the orange trail to the overlook behind Woodcliff Lodge for a wonderful view of the city.)

· Follow the blue trail, turning right at the double blazes. (The red trail goes left.)
· Watch for the double blazes and turn left.
· Duck under a large downed tree.
· At the junction, turn left continuing downhill on the blue trail.
· Emerge into a field with a view of Citibank Corp. below and the Rochester downtown skyline in the distance.
· Follow the field path downhill to the parking lot.

Historical photo of painted stones helping early pilots find their way to Rochester.

Photo courtesy of Larry Fisher

Fishers Park

This park was part of the original Fisher homestead. Long ago, white-washed stones spelling out "Fishers" were placed on the hill to help early airplane pilots find their way to Rochester. Some white stones can still be found on the hill above the present day tennis courts.

This small, quiet, little used park offers picnic tables and charcoal grills at the Main Street entrance, a baseball field at the corner, and tennis courts at the Wangum Road parking lot. Fisherman frequent flowing Irondequoit Creek. Each year additional side trails have been added leading onto private lands. While it may be tempting to venture beyond the park, please respect the landowners rights and stay within the park.

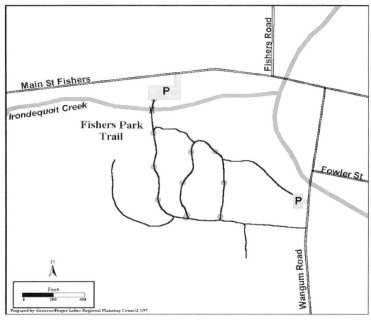

80

16.
Fishers Park Trail

Location:	Fishers Park, Main Street, Fishers (between Wangum Road and Old Dutch Road)
Endpoints:	Fishers Park parking lot
Hiking Time:	45 minutes
Length:	1.5 miles
Difficulty:	👣 👣
Surface:	dirt path
Trail Markings:	none
Uses:	🚶 🎣
Park Size:	37.5 acres
Contact:	Town of Victor
	85 East Main Street
	Victor, NY 14564
	(716) 924-7141

Trail Directions

· Begin at the Main Street parking lot.
· Cross the large bridge over Irondequoit Creek, then cross two smaller bridges.
· Trail continues in the valley and gradually climbs to the top.
· Take the second trail off to the left.
· At the "Y" junction bear left and walk to the next intersection.
· Turn right, retracing your steps back around into the valley and the parking lot.

Ganondagan State Historic Site

Once a major seventeenth-century Seneca town and its palisaded granary, Ganondagan is the only historic site, under the auspices of New York State Office of the Parks, Recreation and Historic Preservation, that is dedicated to Native Americans. The town and its associated burial grounds on Boughton Hill were designated a National Historic Landmark in 1964. Fort Hill, the site of the town's granary, was placed on the National Register of Historic Places in 1966 because it was part of the French campaign of destruction in 1687. The Marquis de Denonville, Governor General of New France, led an army of 3,000 men from Canada against the Seneca in July, 1687, in an effort to annihilate the Seneca and eliminate them as competitors in the international fur trade.

The Seneca Indians recall a much earlier time, when a man referred to as the Peacemaker journeyed to their territory and met a woman known as Mother of Nations or Peace Mother. The Seneca know Ganondagan as the "Town of Peace," and revere and protect the burial site of the Mother of Nations near here.

Interpretive signs on the three main trails within Ganondagan teach the significance of plant life for the Seneca, Seneca customs and beliefs, features of the 30 acre granary at Fort Hill, and the events that took place at the granary. On July 14, 1987, Ganondagan was dedicated - 300 years to the day after Denonville destroyed life at Ganondagan..

The visitors' center features an exhibit describing the Seneca clan system, a display of works by Seneca artists, and a twenty-seven minute video about the history of Ganondagan. The visitors' center and gift shop are open May 15 through October 31, Wednesday through Sunday, 9 a.m. to 5 p.m.

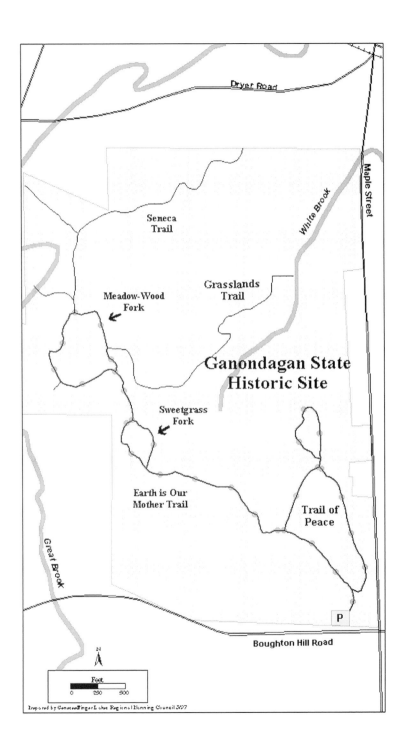

Dryer Road

Maple Street

White Brook

Seneca
Trail

Grasslands
Trail

Meadow-Wood
Fork

**Ganondagan State
Historic Site**

Sweetgrass
Fork

Earth is Our
Mother Trail

Trail of
Peace

Great Brook

P

Boughton Hill Road

N

Feet
0   250   500

Prepared by Genesee/Finger Lakes Regional Planning Council 2007

17.
Trail Of Peace

Location:	Ganondagan State Historic Site, Boughton Hill Road, Victor
Endpoints:	Ganondagan parking lot on Boughton Hill at the corner of Victor-Holcomb Road
Hiking Time:	30 minutes
Length:	0.4 mile
Difficulty:	
Surface:	wide mowed grass path in an open field
Trail Markings:	baked-enamel and metal interpretive signs line the trail
Uses:	
Contact:	Ganondagan State Historic Site
P.O. Box 239
1488 Victor-Holcomb Road
Victor, NY 14564-0239
(716) 924-5848

84

Trail Of Peace

Trail Directions

· From the parking lot head north across a mowed grass area toward an interpretive sign.

· Turn left down the 6-foot wide mowed path.

· At the first junction turn right, staying on the mowed path.

· If you keep bearing left at each junction and stay on the wide mowed path, the trail will loop back to the beginning. Along the way, be sure to take time to enjoy the interpretive signs.

18.
Earth Is Our Mother Trail

Location:	Ganondagan State Historic Site, Boughton Hill Road, Victor
Endpoints:	Ganondagan parking lot on Boughton Hill Road at the corner of Victor-Holcomb Road
Hiking Time:	1.5 hours
Length:	2 miles
Difficulty:	👣 👣 👣
Surface:	dirt path with boardwalks
Trail Markings:	29 baked-enamel and stainless-steel interpretive signs
Uses:	🚶
Contact:	Ganondagan State Historic Site
	P.O. Box 239
	1488 Victor-Holcomb Road
	Victor, NY 14564-0239
	(716) 924-5848

Trail Directions

NOTE: Follow the main trail (green blaze) outbound to Great Brook. Then return taking the Meadow-Wood Fork and Sweetgrass Fork.

· From the parking lot head north across a mowed grass area toward an interpretive sign.

· Turn left down the 6-foot wide mowed path following the Trail of Peace.

· At the first junction continue straight, heading into a high brush woods. The next interpretive sign will identify this as an ethnobotanical trail.

· The trail will descend several flights of steps.

· Cross a boardwalk. (Wet area in spring.)

· Continue straight through the first junction. (A trail to the left takes you to an interpretive sign.)

· Cross another boardwalk.

· At the Sweetgrass Fork, turn left. (Straight is part of the return leg of the hike.)

· At the junction turn left again.

· Cross three boardwalks

· At the junction continue straight.

· Cross one boardwalk.

· At the junction turn right. (Note: If you wish, continue straight for 50 feet. Then the trail has another junction. Turning left takes you to Great Brook and a beautiful cascading stream. Continuing straight takes you to the beginning of Victor Hiking Trail's 5.8-mile long Seneca Trail.)

· Exit woods. Continue straight. (Grassland Trail, a 2-mile linear trail, enters from the left.)

· Trail reenters woods. At the junction turn left (S) and cross three boardwalks.

· At the Sweetgrass Fork turn left up hill.

· At the four-way juncture continue straight ahead (S).

· Emerge onto the mowed trail portion. Continue straight then bear right to return to the parking lot.

"The world is a book, and those who do not travel read only a page."

Saint Augustine

19.
Fort Hill Trail

Endpoints:	grass parking lot on Boughton Hill Road
Location:	Boughton Hill Road, Victor (near corner of Murray Road)
Hiking Time:	1 hour
Length:	0.9 mile
Difficulty:	
Surface:	dirt path and mowed grass path
Trail Markings:	interpretive signs
Uses:	
Contact:	Ganondagan State Historic Site P.O. Box 239 1488 Victor-Holcomb Road Victor, NY 14564-0239 (716) 924-5848

Trail Directions

· From the parking lot head uphill on the mowed path.

· The trail turns right and enters the woods through wooden fence posts.

· Cross a boardwalk. To your left note the marsh area, once a spring used by the Seneca.

· Emerge to a mowed field at the top of the hill. (A small trail off to the right goes to private property.)

· Head straight into the field. The mowed path will make a loop around the top of the plateau. Follow signs to stay on the main trail.

· At the end of the loop, turn right at the junction (watch for "trail" sign) and retrace your steps down the same trail to the parking lot.

89

Highland Park

This was Monroe County's first public park, dedicated in 1890 to the children of Rochester. The park began as a dream of two nurserymen, George Ellwanger and Patrick Barry who proposed the park and donated 20 acres of their nursery grounds to the city. Famous for its collections of magnolia, horse chestnut, barberry, Japanese maple, rhododendron, and lilac (more than 1200), Highland Park is one of the oldest public arboretums or "tree gardens" in the United States.

Here are the best times to view various flowering plants:

mid-April	forsythia
late-April	magnolia
early-May	tulip
mid-May	flowering dogwood
late-May	azalea
	lilac
	pansy bed
	wisteria
early-June	rhododendron
July	hydrangea

While enjoying the park, don't miss the Lamberton Conservatory, a landmark in Highland Park since 1911. Within the glass walls of the Conservatory, located on Reservoir Avenue, are a wonderful tropical forest area, exotic plants, desert plants, plants with economic uses such as banana and coffee trees, and seasonal floral displays. Exhibits are changed five times throughout the year.

Conservatory Hours:

May through October	
Wednesday	10 a.m. to 8 p.m.
Thursday through Sunday	10 a.m. to 6 p.m.
November through April	
Wednesday through Sunday	10 a.m. to 4 p.m.
Closed Monday and Tuesday	

90

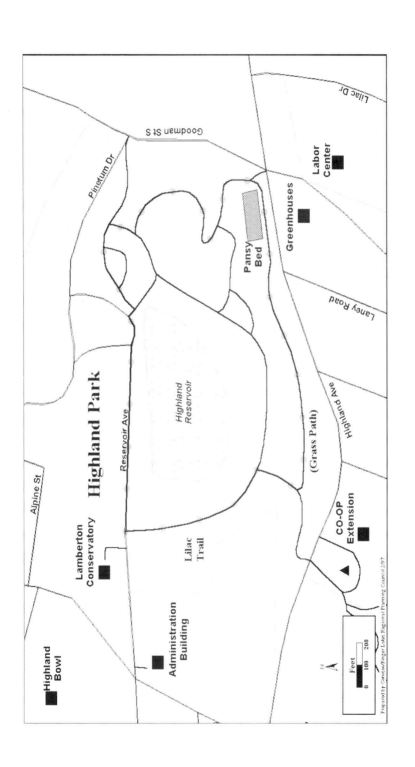

Highland Park

Highland Bowl

Alpine St

Lamberton Conservatory

Administration Building

Pinetum Dr

Reservoir Ave

Highland Reservoir

Lilac Trail

Goodman St S

Pansy Bed

Greenhouses

(Grass Path)

Highland Ave

Laney Road

CO-OP Extension

Labor Center

Lilac Dr

N

Feet
0   100   200

Prepared by Genesee/Finger Lakes Regional Planning Council 2/97

20.

Lilac Trail

Location:	Highland Park, Rochester
Endpoints:	park along Reservoir Avenue, near the Lamberton Conservatory
Hiking Time:	30 minutes
Length:	0.8 mile
Difficulty:	
Surface:	paved path and grass path
Uses:	
Trail Markings:	signs
Park Size:	150 acres
Contact:	Monroe County Parks Department
	171 Reservoir Avenue
	Rochester, NY 14620
	(716) 256-4950

Trail Directions

· From the conservatory, walk east along Reservoir Avenue until you reach the old stone reservoir building.
· Take a right on the paved walkway, then bear left past the overlook area.
· Head down a flight of stairs and bear right. (Straight is a good side trip to take if the azaleas and rhododendrons are in bloom.)
· Make a sharp left turn and head downhill.

⬤ 👣 Lilac Trail

· Follow the paved path as it winds downhill.
· Continue straight when a path leads off to the right.
· At the base of the hill, just before Highland Avenue, turn right and head west along Highland Avenue.
· Pass the pansy bed and continue west along a grass path through the lilac bushes.
· Take a right when you meet the paved walkway and head uphill.
· At the next junction turn left and pass through the magnolia trees.
· This walkway will take you back to Reservoir Avenue.

Mendon Ponds Park

This is another jewel in the county's park system, filled with lakes, woods, and rolling hills. Mendon Ponds Park is the largest park in Monroe County and was designated a National Natural Landmark because of its unique glacial land forms.

The park's geologic features were formed by the last of four major glaciers that covered the area 12,000 to 14,000 years ago. The glacier reached to the Pennsylvania border and was 5,000 to 10,000 feet thick. As the ice melted, large amounts of sand, rock, and gravel were deposited. Three main geologic features visible in the park today are kames, eskers, and kettles.

Kames- formed by rivers that flowed on top of the glacier and spilled over the edge depositing soil into huge piles.

KAME

Eskers- formed when rivers flowed under the glacier in an ice tunnel. Rocky material accumulated on the tunnel beds, and when the glacier melted, a ridge of rubble remained.

ESKER

94

Kettles- created when a large block of ice separated from the glacier. Water running off of the glacier deposited gravel and debris all around the ice block. The block melted, leaving behind a rough circular depression.

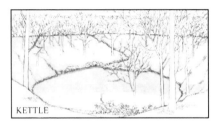

KETTLE

People from all over the country come to study "Devil's Bathtub." This kettle is a rare meromictic lake, of which there are only a few in the world. A meromictic lake is a very deep body of water surrounded by high ridges. Because the high ridges prevent the wind from blowing on the water, a motionless surface gives the lake a mirrored effect.

The first inhabitants of this area were the Algonquin, Iroquois, and Seneca Indians who left behind many Indian trails. On July 23, 1687, Denonville's army used the trails to invade the Indians in the region. In his memoirs, Denonville recalls looking down from the top of one of the ridges at "three pretty little lakes." This marks the first reference to Mendon Ponds in our recorded history. The first white settler in the Mendon Ponds area was Joshua Lillie, who is buried on a small plot on Wilmarth Road. The park was dedicated in 1928 and now has 25 to 30 miles of winding trails.

Don't forget to stop by the nature center for a map on additional trails and information on the glacial geology of the park. The center offers weekly family programs at various county parks and is open Thursday through Sunday, noon until 4:00 p.m., telephone (716) 334-3780.

21.
Birdsong Trail

Location:	Mendon Ponds Park, Mendon (Clover Street / Route 65)
Endpoints:	Nature Center on Pond Road
Hiking Time:	25 minutes
Length:	1 mile
Difficulty:	
Surface:	wide and level farm lane
Uses:	(pets are not allowed)
Trail Markings:	signs
Park Size:	2,550 acres
Contact:	Monroe County Parks Department
	171 Reservoir Avenue
	Rochester, NY 14620
	(716) 256-4950

As the name indicates, many birds populate this area especially black-capped chickadees. These friendly, curious creatures will fly right up to you, and if you have sunflower seeds, they will eat out of your hand in the winter. Birdsong Trail is a wide farm lane that has many labeled trees and easy-to-follow signs.

Trail Directions
· Begin at the arbor walkway, then bear left.

96

Birdsong Trail

· Bear right at the first junction.
· Follow the signs for "Birdsong Trail."
· A side trail takes you around a small swamp with an observation deck
  and benches.
· Follow the sign at the junction and turn right to return to the Nature
  Center. (Left takes you to the Swamp Trail.)

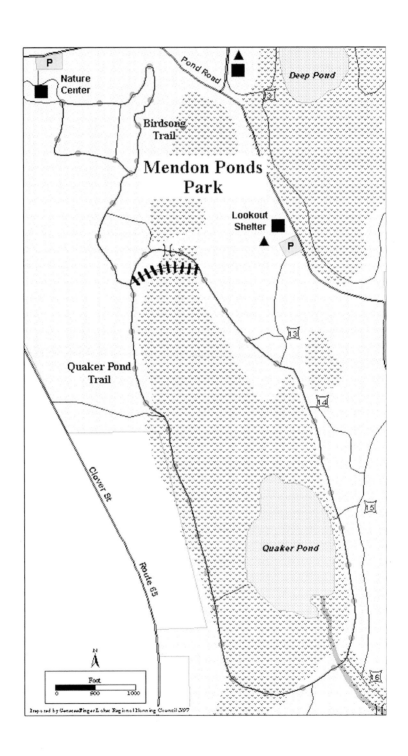

P

Nature
Center

Pond Road

Deep Pond

Birdsong
Trail

Mendon Ponds
Park

Lookout
Shelter

P

Quaker Pond
Trail

Clover St

Route 65

Quaker Pond

N

Feet

0   500   1000

Prepared by Genesee/Finger Lakes Regional Planning Council 2007

22.
Quaker Pond Trail

Location:	Mendon Ponds, Mendon (Clover Street / Route 65)
Endpoints:	Nature Center on Pond Road
Hiking Time:	1.5 hours
Length:	3.5 miles
Difficulty:	
Surface:	mowed grass path
Uses:	(pets are not allowed)
Trail Markings:	signs
Park Size:	2,550 acres
Contact:	Monroe County Parks Department
	171 Reservoir Avenue
	Rochester, NY 14620
	(716) 256-4950

This trail offers great views of the pond that contains beaver houses and a variety of waterfowl. It's a fun place to identify animal tracks (deer, raccoon, etc.) in the mud. You can make the hike even longer by following any of the numerous side trails. Note the alternate entrance to the trail via the Lookout Shelter parking area off Pond Road.

Quaker Pond Trail

Trail Directions

· Begin at the arbor walkway, then bear left.

· Bear right at the first junction following Birdsong Trail to the Swamp Trail signs. This leads you to Quaker Pond Trail.

· Follow the signs for "Quaker Pond Trail."

· On the return leg be sure to take the side trail off to the left leading to a boardwalk through the swamp.

· At the juncture turn right following the signs for "Return to Nature Center."

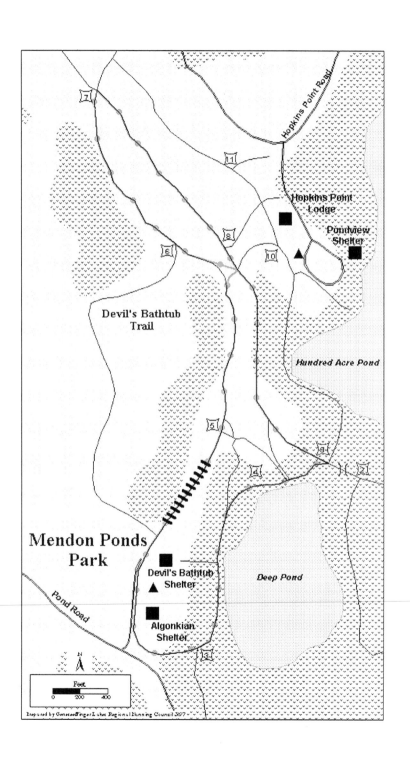

Hopkins Point Road

⟨7⟩

⟨11⟩

Hopkins Point Lodge

Pondview Shelter

⟨8⟩

⟨6⟩

⟨10⟩

Devil's Bathtub Trail

Hundred Acre Pond

⟨5⟩

⟨9⟩

⟨4⟩

⟨2⟩

Mendon Ponds Park

Devil's Bathtub Shelter

Deep Pond

Pond Road

Algonkian Shelter

⟨3⟩

N

Feet
0   200   400

Prepared by Genesee/Finger Lakes Regional Planning Council 2007

23.
Devil's Bathtub Trail

Location:	Mendon Ponds Park, Mendon (Clover Street / Route 65)
Endpoints:	Algonkian Shelter parking lot on Pond Road
Hiking Time:	1 hour
Length:	1.9 miles
Difficulty:	👣 👣 👣
Surface:	dirt path
Uses:	
Trail Markings:	signs
Park Size:	2,550 acres
Contact:	Monroe County Parks Department
	171 Reservoir Avenue
	Rochester, NY 14620
	(716) 256-4950

This hike offers an excellent view of a kettle and an esker. It has varied, moderate ascents and descents, one using stairs.

Trail Directions
· Follow the paved Devil's Bathtub Shelter access road uphill. (The road is closed to cars in the winter.)
· At the top go to the wooden "Devil's Bathtub" sign.

102

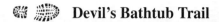 **Devil's Bathtub Trail**

· Descend the wooden stairs and continue straight on the boardwalk.
· At the next two junctions continue straight ahead and then ascend the esker.
· At the crest turn right (SE) following an old park lane along the crest. You are now doubling back looking down on where you just were.
· At junction marker "8" continue straight. Hundred Acre Pond is on your left in the distance.
· There are several side trails, but stay on the 6-foot wide main trail which eventually descends off the ridge.
· At junction marker "9" turn right. You are now walking beside Deep Pond.
· Stay on the main trail as it follows the edge of the pond until you are back at the Algonkian Shelter parking area.

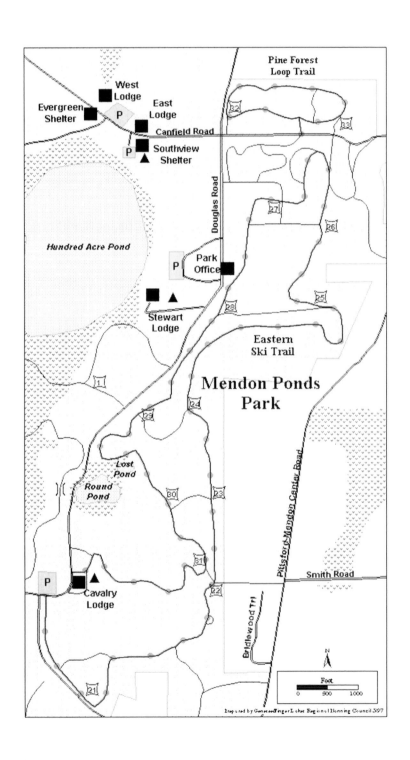

Pine Forest
Loop Trail

West Lodge

Evergreen Shelter

P

East Lodge

Canfield Road

P

Southview Shelter

Douglas Road

32

33

27

26

Hundred Acre Pond

P

Park Office

25

Stewart Lodge

28

Eastern
Ski Trail

**Mendon Ponds
Park**

1

24

29

Lost Pond

Round Pond

30

23

31

P

Cavalry Lodge

22

Smith Road

Pittsford-Mendon Center Road

Bridlewood Trl

21

N

Feet

0   500   1000

Prepared by Genesee/Finger Lakes Regional Planning Council 1997

24.
Eastern Ski Trail

Location:	Mendon Ponds Park, Mendon (Clover Street / Route 65)
Endpoints:	parking lot at the corner of Pond Road and Douglas Road
Hiking Time:	2.5 hours
Length:	6.2 miles
Difficulty:	👣 👣 👣
Surface:	dirt path
Uses:	🎿 🎿
Trail Markings:	not well marked, some blue and white metal signs on wooden posts at trail junctions
Park Size:	2,550 acres
Contact:	Monroe County Parks Department
	171 Reservoir Avenue
	Rochester, NY 14620
	(716) 256-4950

This wide, distinctive hilly path through the woods is used for cross-country skiing in the winter. There are many opportunities to shorten the loop hike, if you wish.

Trail Directions

· From the parking lot, cross Douglas Road and walk parallel (S) along the wide mowed grass area next to Pond Road for 10 minutes. Just before Add-En-On Kennels, note a gravel ramp with two posts designating a horse trailer parking area in the lawn.

· Turn left (N) and follow the farm lane with a single wooden rail fence line.

· Continue uphill on the main path avoiding the cutoff on the left.

· Go up and over the crest.

· At the "Y" junction, bear left and go up the hill.

· At the top of the hill is a tiny loop with a view and picnic table. Continue on, observing the "Stay on Trail" sign.

· Go over Duck Hill (sign on top) and at junction marker "22," continue straight on the path marked for hiking. Note: A horse trail parallels and crosses the hiking trail a few times.

· At the top of the next hill at junction marker "23," continue straight, up and down several hills to junction marker "24."

· Bear right and ascend and then descend an esker.

· Continue straight at the unmarked junction.

· Trail winds up a steep hill past power lines and a cement water tower.

· Path continues on the opposite side of the tower using a gravel road for a short distance.

· At junction "25" turn right down a wood chip path.

· At junction "26" bear right.

· At the top of the hill juncture continue straight.

· For the next several unmarked junctions, always bear left. (Notice trees that were planted in rows.)

· At junction "27" continue straight. Also continue straight through an unmarked junction.

· Cross the lawn behind the park office building and reenter woods.

· Turn right on the gravel road (left goes to cement water tower) and turn left at the gated fence.

· After several hills enter grass area following the line of the woods and reenter the woods to the left after 1,000 feet.

· At the "Y" bear right heading toward Douglas Road.

· Follow trail as it bears left, then up a hill to a sharp right.

⚜ 🐾 Eastern Ski Trail

· Trail bends left as you approach Douglas Road.
· At the picnic area follow the ski signs to the left around Lost Pond area, returning into the woods.
· At junction "30" continue straight. The path is leaf covered and the terrain is gentle through this area.
· At junction "31" turn right, uphill. The area gets hilly again.
· At the next juncture follow the widest trail (right).
· Follow the dirt road left to Cavalry Lodge.
· Cross Douglas Road to the mowed grass field and the parking lot on the left.

Bonus: Pine Forest Loop Trail

This is a delightful 30 minutes (1.2 miles) around a mature pine forest using a wide country lane. The trail makes a big rectangle with a shortcut trail through the center.

Trail Directions
· Park on the north side of Canfield Road between Douglas Road and Mendon Center Road. A yellow pipe gate set back near the woods is the entrance.
· Walk to the opening in the woods on the north side of the road.
· Since this is a loop, you can take the trail in either direction.

Powder Mills Park

Set in steep, wooded hills, Powder Mills Park offers downhill and cross-country skiing in the winter. Fishing in Irondequoit Creek and the fish hatchery are favorite attractions in the summer.

Development of the area began in 1850 when Daniel C. Rand arrived from Middletown, Connecticut, where he worked as a manufacturer of blasting powder.

Rand came to this area and chose a small, ideal spot, far enough from settlements, but still close to the Erie Canal. In 1852 Rand, in partnership with Mortimer Wadhams, opened his mill for making blasting powder, and called it the Rand & Wadhams Powder Company.

The process for making blasting powder, which is simply a course version of gun powder, had been known for 100 years and involves grinding and mixing saltpeter (potassium nitrate), sulfur, and charcoal. To be an effective explosive, the ingredients have to be ground to an extremely fine consistency.

Irondequoit Creek was dammed to create a pond and a millrace for power to turn the great grinding stones and other machines used to pulverize the ingredients of blasting power. But it was a dangerous job. While in Connecticut, Rand had witnessed several accidents and his attention was drawn to the Rochester area by news of explosions that destroyed some powder mills in Allens Creek.

During construction of his new mill, Rand took several measures to help prevent or lessen the consequences of possible explosions. First, each step of the process was performed in a separate building so an explosion in one would not send the whole business up in flames.

Rand also sought to eliminate sparks due to metal touching metal. The buildings were connected by a narrow-gage railroad with wooden rails on which rode small cars with wooden wheels. And employees were not allowed to have any metal in their clothing. Many men even wore felt-soled slippers because their regular boots were constructed with nails.

Finally, to lessen the chance of fires or vandalism, Rand kept the property off limits to all hunting, fishing, and camping. This created the air of mystery about the area that lingered years after the mills were gone. In the 58 years of operation, several small explosions and two injuries occurred at the mill, but no catastrophic explosions or deaths.

Rand bought saltpeter and sulfur, but made his own charcoal out of willow trees that grew abundantly in the valley. Over the years Rand planted hundreds of new willows to replace those he cut. The willow was burned very slowly to produce charcoal. The charcoal and sulfur were ground together, with the saltpeter being ground separately. After both were reduced to course grain, they were combined and ground together for several hours. They were then formed into large cakes under 3,000 to 4,000 pounds pressure. The cakes in turn were re-ground with graphite, which made the powder flow better. The powder was then sieved to different grades and packed in 25-pound kegs, with the finest being the most powerful blasting powder.

Rand died in 1883 and his partner passed on three years later. Rand's two sons, Mortimer and Samuel, continued the mill operation under the name D.C. Rand Powder Co. The brothers quit the business in 1910 and moved to Uniontown, Pennsylvania, to set up another mill closer to the coal mines that consumed the powder.

The property and buildings were left vacant until 1929 when 290 acres were purchased by the Monroe County Parks Commission. At that time the mill and homestead were razed.

25.
Irondequoit Creek Trail

Location:	Powder Mills Park, (Interstate 490 exit Bushnell's Basin, left Route 96 (S), right on Park Road, left on Corduroy Road, right on Woolston Road)
Endpoints:	gravel parking lot on south side of Woolston Road near Oak Tree Shelter
Hiking Time:	45 minutes
Length:	1.5 miles
Difficulty:	
Surface:	dirt path
Trail Markings:	blue and white metal signs on wooden posts at trail junctions
Uses:	
Park Size:	380 acres
Contact:	Monroe County Parks Department
	171 Reservoir Avenue
	Rochester, NY 14620
	(716) 256-4950

Irondequoit Creek Trail

Trail Directions

· Head down Woolston Road (E) away from Oak Tree Shelter. The trail entrance will be on the right (across Woolston Road is marker "6.") Enter trail marked "Most Difficult."
· At junction "15" bear right. Cross a stream.
· At "T" junction "14" turn left and climb a hill.
· Keep left at the grassy bowl area.
· At junction "13" bear right and head uphill.
· At junction "12" turn left to a gradual uphill. Pass several trails off to the right. Pass through a small patch of horsetails.
· The trail bends right. A ravine is on your left. The trail continues bending right with a trail entering from the right.
· Pass through a second small patch of horsetails. Eventually, Irondequoit Creek will be on your left.
· After a short uphill, turn right at the yellow vehicle barricade and continue on a gradual uphill. (Straight ahead goes to brown park buildings.)
· At each trail junction bear right until you reach junction "12." Turn left and head downhill. At the bottom of the bowl, continue downhill.
· At junction "14" go straight. (Trail to right crosses a stream.)
· Follow the woodchip path to the parking lot.

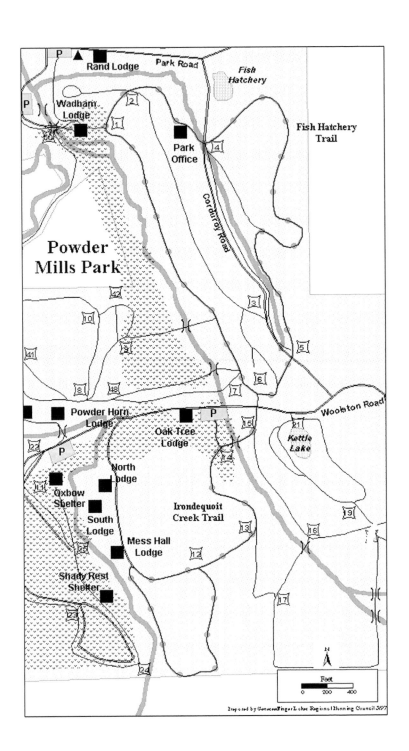

26.
Fish Hatchery Trail

Location:	Powder Mills Park, (Interstate 490 exit Bushnell's Basin, left Route 96 (S), right on Park Road, left on Corduroy Road, right on WoolstonRoad)
Endpoints:	gravel parking lot is on south side of Woolston Road near Oak Tree Shelter
Hiking Time:	45 minutes
Length:	1.5 miles
Difficulty:	👣 👣 👣
Surface:	dirt path
Trail Markings:	blue and white metal signs on wooden posts at trail junctions
Uses:	
Park Size:	380 acres
Contact:	Monroe County Parks Department 171 Reservoir Avenue Rochester, NY 14620 (716) 256-4950

Trail Directions

· Cross Woolston Road to marker "7" and the "Easiest Ski" trail sign. Enter woods.

· At junction "1" take a right and go uphill.

113

SIDE TRIP TO MILL WHEEL: From junction "1" bear left. Go past Wadham's Shelter and cross a bridge over the creek. Mill Wheel is in a fenced in area on the right. Return to junction "1."

· At the top of the hill bear right. (To the left is a small side loop trail.)
· At junction "2" bear left.

SIDE TRIP TO FISH HATCHERY: Near the bottom of hill is a trail to the left leading to the fish hatchery.

· Proceed to parking lot of yellow park office building, turn left and cross the bridge.
· Cross Corduroy Road and proceed straight ahead to junction "4."
· Enter woods and start uphill.
· After awhile the trail bends to the right, then it meanders left and right.
· Watch for an extreme sharp left turn as you head downhill. (If you miss this turn you'll end up at the road near the yellow park office building again.)
· Trail levels out at base of hill. At a "T" junction turn right.
· At junction "5" cross Corduroy Road and turn right.
· After 15 yards reenter the woods on the left.
· At the road turn right and follow the road back to the parking lot.

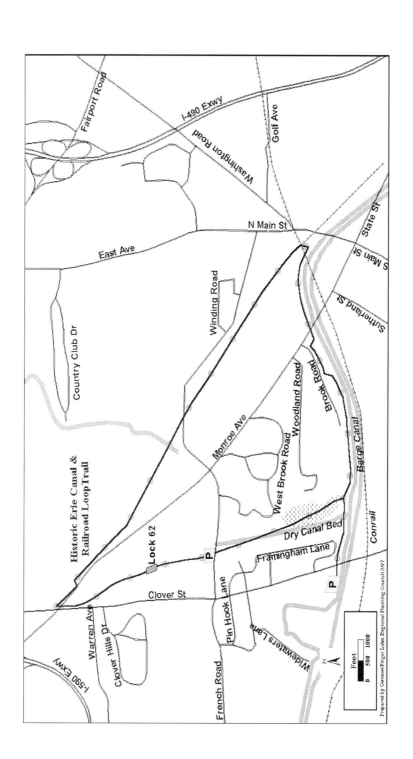

Historic Erie Canal & Railroad Loop Trail

27.
Historic Erie Canal and Railroad Loop Trail

Location:	Lock #32 Canal Park, Pittsford (Clover Street / Route 65)
Endpoints:	Lock #32 Canal Park parking area
Hiking Time:	2.5 hours
Length:	4 miles
Difficulty:	
Surface:	mowed grass path, paved path
Trail Markings:	none
Uses:	
Contact:	Pittsford Parks Department
	35 Lincoln Avenue
	Pittsford, NY 14534
	(716) 248-6280

Erie Canal & Railroad Loop Trail

As the name of the trail implies, you will be hiking on not one but two historic paths of transportation. The original Erie Canal headed north from here to Rochester and that route is now Interstates 390 and 490. Along the way you'll see signs of the World War II Odenbach Shipyard, where landing craft were made, and Lock #62 built in 1855. Then it's on to the Rochester and Auburn railbed, an active railroad from 1840 through 1960. Both of these sections are maintained by the Pittsford Parks Department and the Pittsford Trails Coalition. The third leg of the trip takes you along the present day Erie Canal for a scenic walk back to Lock #32 Canal Park.

Trail Directions
· Begin by heading east on the paved canal towpath crossing underneath Route 65.
· Turn left (N) at the map post showing the "Historic Erie Canal & Railroad Loop Trail."
· As you're walking on the 20-foot wide grass path, notice the remains of the old canal bed on your left.
· Cross French Road and the trail parking area. The trail narrows to 6 feet.
· The rear of Pittsford Plaza emerges. Note: The access trail is between Wegman's parking and plaza parking.
· Dual Lock #32 is on your left.
· Follow the trail down steps and then over a small wooden bridge.
· Turn right after bridge. (Trail to the left goes to homes.)
· Now you're walking on the old canal bed. Trail narrows to 3 feet.
· Trail exits at the Spring House Restaurant parking lot.
· Walk to the corner of Clover Street and cross Monroe Avenue. Be sure to use the crosswalk on this busy street.
· Walk east on Monroe Avenue. The trail begins again behind the Park Avenue Bike Shop. This next segment of the trail is on the old Rochester and Auburn railbed.
· The trail passes behind many buildings on Monroe Avenue. A store that you may want to stop at is the Pittsford Ice Cream and Cakes Store.
· Cross French Road.

117

- As you approach a commercial storage building, the trail to the right leads through village woods to Pittsford Village DPW service road, which leads to the canal towpath. Or, you may continue straight on the path beside the storage building to the Pickle Factory and village.
- At the canal towpath, turn right (E) to Canal Park Lock #32.
- Note: Follow the canal trail signs around NYS Canal Maintenance property.

Southwest
Section

"There are many paths to the top of the mountain, but the view is always the same."

Chinese Proverb

Black Creek Park

Black Creek is the centerpiece of this park in southwestern Monroe County. Purchased in 1963, the park has large tracts of undeveloped, rolling hills with two small ponds. Its trails wind through tall brush and young forest areas. Six-foot wide paths are mowed throughout the park creating many possible hiking or cross-country skiing loops. Deer are plentiful in the park.

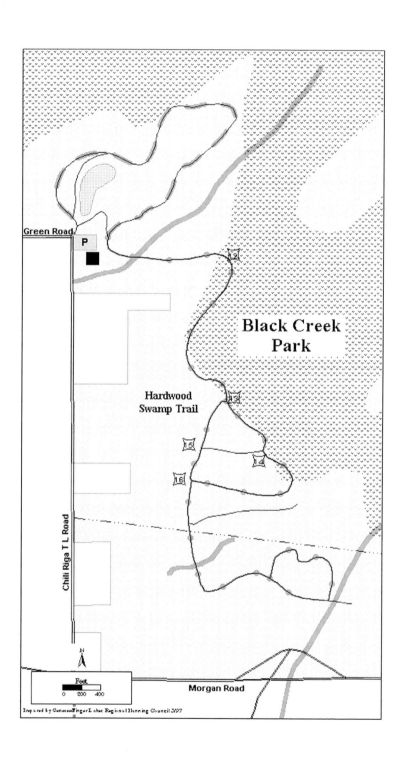

Green Road

P

Black Creek
Park

Hardwood
Swamp Trail

Chili Riga T L Road

N

Feet
0   200   400

Morgan Road

Prepared by Genesee/Finger Lakes Regional Planning Council 2007

28.
Hardwood Swamp Trail

Location:	Black Creek Park, Chili-Riga Town Line Road, Chili (off Route 33A)
Endpoints:	parking lot at corners of Green Road and Chili-Riga Town Line Road
Hiking Time:	75 minutes
Length:	2.5 miles
Difficulty:	👣 👣
Surface:	mowed grass path
Trail Markings:	junctions are marked with blue-and-white numbered signs on wooden posts
Uses:	🚶 🚴 🐎
Park Size:	1,505 acres
Contact:	Monroe County Parks Department 171 Reservoir Avenue Rochester, NY 14620 (716) 256-4950

Trail Directions

· From the parking lot, bear right (S) past the red barn. At a wide grassy area turn left to find the beginning of the trail.

· Cross the bridge over a small creek and at junction "12" bear left on the main trail. (Off to the right is a small side trail.)

· Junction "13" is a "Y." Bear right for a gradual uphill walk.

123

· Bear right at junction "15."
· Go straight (right) at junction "16."
· The next junction is an unmarked "Y." Power lines are directly in front of you. Bear right under the power lines. Cross a low area which may have a running stream in wet times of the year.
· The trail parallels the power lines. (They're on your left.)
· At the next "Y" junction bear left to stay on the mowed path. (Straight ahead is access for maintenance vehicles.)
· Pass under the power lines. Shortly at another "Y" bear right and start uphill, remaining under the power lines.
· After a downhill, you'll see a gravel area with an old bridge over a creek straight ahead. This is a dead end. (Future plans indicate it will continue.) Turn left and loop back under the power lines.
· The trail meanders up and down hills and wanders left and right.
· Turn right at the next junction and you are back on the trail you were on previously. Cross the wet lowland again.
· At the next junction go straight (left). (The trail to the right is a dead end.) Note the old stone fence in the wooded area.
· At junction "16" turn right.
· Bear right at junctions "14" and "13." Pass another old stone fence line. A small path leads off to the left but stay on the main trail.
· A left at junction "12" takes you back to the parking lot.

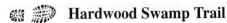 **Hardwood Swamp Trail**

Bonus:

If you would like to explore this part of the park more, try this one mile field loop. It has a mowed grass path and takes only about 25 minutes.

Trail Directions
· From the far end of the parking lot, turn left and cross the grassy area (red barn on your right). A manmade pond is visible to your left.
· Follow the mowed path to the right heading away from the pond. The forest is on your right and a field on your left.
· The mowed path takes you around the perimeter of the field, always with woods to your right. You end up back at the pond.
· At the pond, bear right and cross the grass covered dike.
· Bear right at the "Y" junction, the pond is now below you to the left. (The left trail at this junction takes you to the same end point but follows closer to the pond.)
· The trail ends at the south end of the pond.
· Walk back to the parking lot.

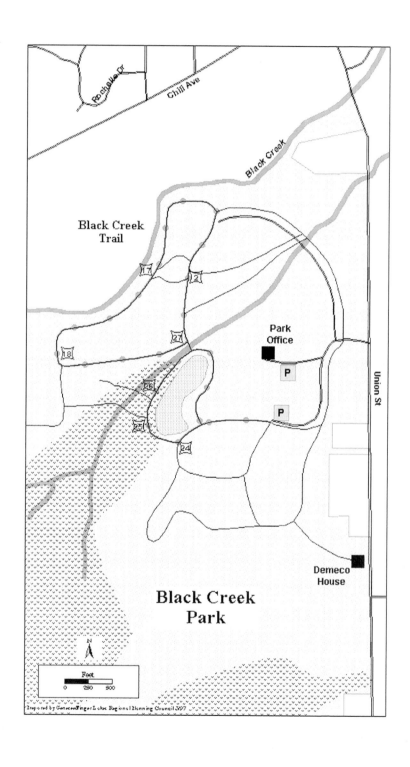

29.
Black Creek Trail

Location:	Black Creek Park, Union Street, Chili (off Route 259)
Endpoints:	parking lot off Union Street
Hiking Time:	60 minutes
Length:	2.0 miles
Difficulty:	👣 👣
Surface:	mowed grass path
Trail Markings:	junctions are marked with blue-and-white numbered signs on wooden posts
Uses:	
Park Size:	1,505 acres
Contact:	Monroe County Parks Department 171 Reservoir Avenue Rochester, NY 14620 (716) 256-4950

Trail Directions

· From the parking lot head down a gravel path toward the yellow metal gate.

· Several mowed paths lead to the pond. Take the one on the far left and proceed along the edge of the woods.

· Keep the woods to your left as you circle the pond, passing junctions "24," "25," and "26."

127

· Cross the pond outlet (may be a few inches deep at wet times of the year).

· Just after the outlet turn left onto a well-used, unmarked path and cross a wooden bridge.

· At the "Y" junction labeled "27," turn left.

· At junction "18" go right (N). The path will bend right and follow Black Creek. At this point you're high on a bank with the creek far below.

· Keep following the creek past trails entering from the right- one an unmarked trail, the other marked "17."

· The trail wanders down to creek level and widens into a mowed picnic area. Keeping the creek to your left, cross the picnic area and follow the path uphill.

· At the top of the hill, continue straight ahead toward a yellow metal gate at the end of a paved road.

· Pass the gate and follow the wide grass and gravel path.

· Shortly before another yellow metal gate (which is labeled "2") turn left through the tree line and emerge into a field.

· Mowed paths lead left, right, and straight ahead. Go straight, past another trail entering from the left.

· At marker "27" turn left and cross the wooden bridge (the same one you crossed on the way out).

· Turn left at the pond and cross the field toward the yellow metal gate.

· The parking lot is just beyond the yellow metal gate.

Genesee Valley Greenway

The Genesee Valley Greenway is a 90-mile historic and natural resource corridor that follows a transportation route used by the Genesee Valley Canal from 1840 to 1878 and later by the railroad from 1880 to the mid 1960s. The former railbed now serves as a multi-use greenway trail. Currently 16 miles of the total 90 miles is open for use.

The trail will eventually connect with the Rochester River Trail, the Erie Canal Heritage Trail, the Finger Lakes Trail, the Allegheny County River Trail, as well as Rochester's Genesee Valley Park and Letchworth State Park.

Development of the first 50 miles from Rochester south to Letchworth is scheduled for completion by the end of 1998. The trail is open for use in the Monroe County village of Scottsville and the towns of Chili and Wheatland. Also open are sections in the Livingston County village of Mt. Morris and the towns of Nunda and Portage. Trail sections in the Livingston County towns of Caledonia, York, Leicester, and Mt. Morris are scheduled to open by the end of 1997.

129

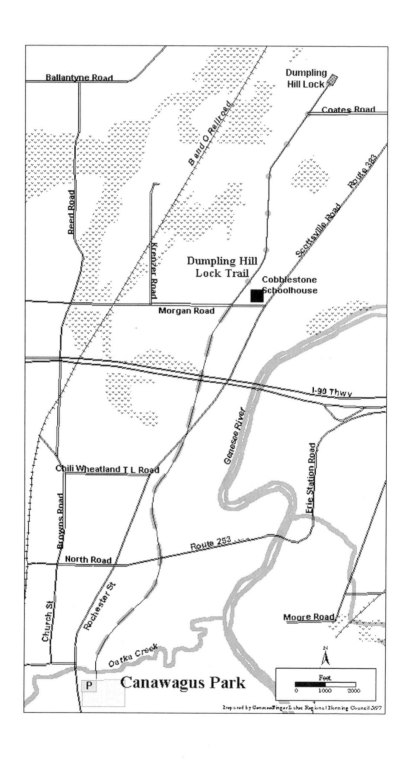

Ballantyne Road

Dumpling
Hill Lock

Coates Road

B and O Railroad

Route 383

Reed Road

Scottsville Road

Krenzer Road

Dumpling Hill
Lock Trail

Cobblestone
Schoolhouse

Morgan Road

I-90 Thwy

Genesee River

Erie Station Road

Chili Wheatland T L Road

Browns Road

Route 253

North Road

Rochester St

Moore Road

Church St

Oatka Creek

P Canawagus Park

N

Feet

0   1000   2000

Prepared by Genesee/Finger Lakes Regional Planning Council 2007

30.
Dumpling Hill Lock Trail

Location:	Morgan Road, Scottsville (off Route 383)
Endpoints:	Morgan Road
Hiking Time:	1 hour
Length:	2.7 miles
Difficulty:	
Surface:	cinder path
Trail Markings:	none (expected summer 1997)
Uses:	
Contact:	Friends of the Genesee Valley Greenway, Inc.
	16 Chapel Street
	Mount Morris, NY 14510
	(716) 658-2569

This portion of the greenway trail has a destination in mind. It takes you to one of the best preserved locks on the old canal system. The original 115 locks were made of either wood, a combination of wood and stone, or all stone. Over the years the wood rotted and most locks deteriorated or were lost altogether. But this 90-foot long, 15-foot wide lock is all stone and well preserved. Each lock

131

⚙ 🚂 Dumpling Hill Lock Trail

had a lock keeper and sometimes a lock house. The Dumpling Hill Lock had a house which was located west of the canal near Coates Road.

Trail Directions
· Park at the roadside by the greenway crossing.
· Walk NE crossing a dirt pile (auto barrier).
· Pass under two sets of power lines.
· Cross a farm lane, then a second and a third lane.
· Lock will be shortly ahead after the third farm lane.

Bonus:

If you enjoy "walking the rails," try the greenway trail from Canawaugus Park (south of the village of Scottsville, Route 251) to Morgan Road. Round trip is 4.8 miles taking approximately 2 hours.

From the park's parking area look across to the north side of Oatka Creek, a feeder gate for the Genesee Valley Canal is located there. A feeder gate consisted of a lock, dam, and toll house.

Trail Directions
· Begin by crossing the railroad bridge heading northeast on the trail.
· Cross Route 253 and pass Rodney Farms, a thoroughbred horse farm, on the right.
· At Route 383 bear left as a mowed path leads up to the road. Use extreme care in crossing. Be careful that you can see oncoming traffic far enough ahead for a safe crossing.
· Turn right, following the outside shoulder of Route 383.
· On the left side is a small graveyard with the gravestone of Joseph Morgan, a Revolutionary War captain. He is credited for being the first settler in Chili in 1792.
· Watch for the trail on the left heading back into the woods. Hop the guardrail and head downhill.
· Pass under the New York State Thruway.
· Cross a gravel driveway.
· Cross a dirt pile as you approach Morgan Road.
· Retrace your steps back to Canawaugus Park.

Oatka Creek Park

Under this lush, wooded park lies a soft-gray colored rock called gypsum. Gypsum was used by early farmers as fertilizer, later becoming this country's first cement. Today it is used in wallboard for home construction. Chemically, gypsum is calcium sulfate and gradually turns soil sour (or acidic). Because dogwood, azalea, and mosses prefer this type of soil, these types of vegetation abound in Oatka Creek Park.

When the trail nears Oatka Creek, you will notice many pits and mounds, remnants of where workers dug gypsum by hand over 150 years ago. They hauled it to the surface with ropes, loaded it into small carts, and pulled it by mules to a mill nearby. You may also find old grist mill foundations and signs of an early settler's log cabin.

Oatka Creek Park is best known for brown trout fishing in Oatka Creek. And if you enjoy bird watching, this is the place. Watch for downy woodpeckers, flickers, eastern bluebirds and many others.

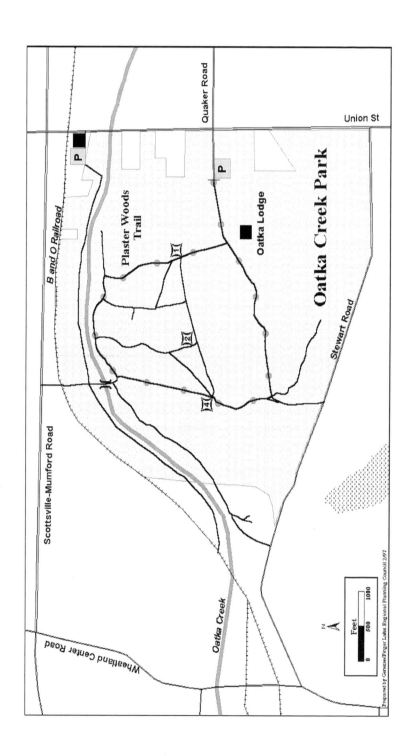

Oatka Creek Park

Plaster Woods Trail

Oatka Lodge

Quaker Road

Union St

B and O Railroad

Scottsville-Mumford Road

Wheatland Center Road

Stewart Road

Oatka Creek

Feet
0 500 1000

Prepared by Genesee/Finger Lakes Regional Planning Council 2/97

31.
Plaster Woods Trail

Location:	Oatka Creek Park, Scottsville (corner of Union Street and Quaker Road)
Endpoints:	parking lot in Oatka Creek Park
Hiking Time:	1 hour
Length:	2 miles
Difficulty:	👣 👣
Surface:	gravel path, mowed grass path, and dirt path
Trail Markings:	none
Park Size:	461 acres, undeveloped
Uses:	🖼️ 🏹 🎿
Contact:	Monroe County Parks Department
	171 Reservoir Avenue
	Rochester, NY 14620
	(716) 256-4950

Trail Directions

· From the parking lot head down the gravel road past Oatka Lodge.

· Turn right (N) just past the yellow guardrails.

· The trail begins wide but soon narrows.

· Continue straight as you pass first one trail, then another trail to your left.

· At the "T" junction turn left following a ridge line above the creek.

· At the next intersection bear right. Here the trail leaves the woods and widens.

· Continue straight. A trail comes in from the left.

135

· At the "Y" junction follow the wide trail to the left. (Trail to the right goes over a concrete farm bridge giving a nice view of the creek.)
· Walk up the hill to where two trails enter from the left. Bear to the right.
· At the "Y" junction bear left. This is quickly followed by a four-way intersection. Turn left onto what once was Quaker Road. Follow this back to the parking lot.

Bonus:

If you would like to see more of this park and Oatka Creek, drive north on Union Street. After passing over the creek look for Ronzo's Grocery on your left, and park in the fisherman's lot behind the store. Follow the path from the southwest corner to the creek. You are able to walk along the creek to the concrete farm bridge and beyond before turning around. Walking this additional section takes about 1.5 hours.

Tinker Nature Park

Donated by the Aldridge family in 1991 and made public in 1994, this well designed park has become a year-round favorite for all ages. The park consists of woods, wetland, ponds, and fields which together create a living museum of natural history. Within the park is the Hansen Nature Center, offering classes in cross-country skiing, snowshoeing, photography, wild flowers, song birds, etc. While there you will also want to visit the Tinker Homestead built in 1830. This cobblestone museum is free and open to the public on Saturdays and Sundays 1 to 4 p.m., other times by appointment.

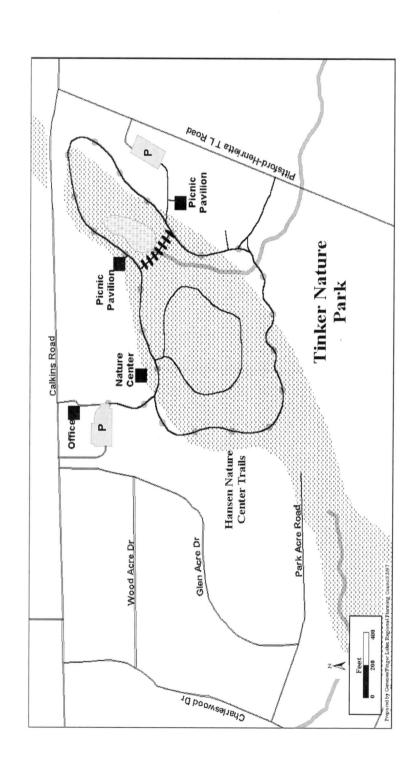

Tinker Nature Park

Hansen Nature Center Trails

Pittsford-Henrietta T.L. Road

Calkins Road

Wood Acre Dr

Glen Acre Dr

Charleswood Dr

Park Acre Road

Office

Nature Center

Picnic Pavilion

Picnic Pavilion

P

P

Feet
0   200   400

N

Prepared by Genesee/Finger Lakes Regional Planning Council 1997

32.
Hansen Nature Center Trails

Location:	1585 Calkins Road, Henrietta (between Pinnacle Road and Henrietta Pittsford Townline Road)
Endpoints:	parking lot
Hiking Time:	45 minutes
Length:	1.2 miles
Difficulty:	
Surface:	gravel path
Trail Markings:	none
Uses:	(pets are not allowed)
Park Size:	68 acres
Contact:	Hansen Nature Center
	P.O. Box 999
	1585 Calkins Road
	Henrietta, NY 14467-0999
	(716) 359-7044
	Tinker Museum (716) 359-7042

Trail Directions

· From the parking lot follow the paved path past the nature center.
· Bear left. (Trail from right is a boardwalk offering a nice view of a pond.)

139

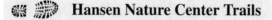

· Continue following the gravel path past a pavilion and picnic area. Boardwalk shortcut rejoins trail.
· Bear right where a side trail from the road enters.
· Wind through woods reemerging in a meadow near the nature center.
· Follow the paved path back to parking lot.

Bonus:

Directly in front of Hansen Nature Center is another 0.5-mile-loop nature trail. This wood-chipped path is worth exploring.

Northwest
Section

"Flowers have spoken to me more than I can tell in written words. They are the hieroglyphics of angels, loved by all men for the beauty of their character, though few can decypher even fragments of their meaning."

Lydia M. Child (1802-80)
U.S. abolitionist, writer, editor

Braddock Bay Raptor Research - Waterfowl Refuge

Come here in the spring to see owls and hawks "up close and personal" in this wetland area.

Upwards of 100,000 hawks, eagles, falcons, and vultures migrate over Braddock Bay along Lake Ontario each spring. This migration of raptors or "birds of prey" offers a unique opportunity to learn a great deal about the birds. One common research technique is capturing, banding, and releasing the birds.

A hawk-banding blind was built in 1984 and is open for visitation. This is the only banding station in North America with an open door policy. However, you must adhere to the following guidelines, or the policy could change.

Policy Guidelines for the Hawk-Banding Area

· Enter only by the back door.
· When you can see the back of the blind, yell "Clear?" and wait for a response. If there is no answer, wait where you are. No response could mean the operators haven't heard you or they are remaining quiet because a hawk is nearby. Try calling again after 30 seconds. If the response is "No," wait until the operator gives you clearance to come in.
· If no one answers please do not enter the area or touch the nets and traps. Do not go out to the traps without permission.
· Ask permission to photograph or videotape any bird or trap.
· Sometimes the blind can become crowded, and the operator will request either that you take only a short look or that you come back at a later time.

From March through May hawks migrate during the day. Owls migrate at night, sleeping in the pine forest and thickets till evening,

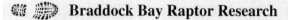

when they continue their journey. The trail wraps around and through this small grouping of pine trees allowing the opportunity to view the birds up close if you're lucky. The most common species of owls you will see is the northern saw-whet, but others such as the long-eared, short-eared, and great-horned have been seen here also. Remember, this area was established to help protect raptors. We are the visitors and should be respectful by being quiet and staying on the established trails.

Also, nearby Braddock Bay Park has a hawk-watch platform for bird spotting. During the spring many people volunteer to count the various species flying high over the Rochester skies. Don't forget to bring your binoculars.

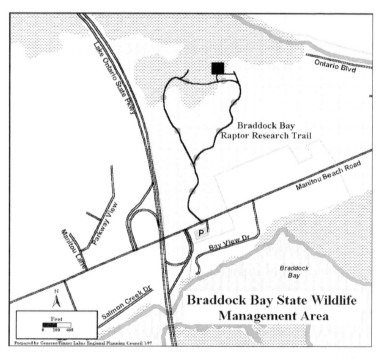

33.
Braddock Bay Raptor Research Trail

Location:	Manitou Beach Road, Hilton (off Lake Ontario State Parkway)
Endpoints:	Manitou Beach Road parking lot
Hiking Time:	30 minutes
Length:	0.5 mile
Difficulty:	
Surface:	woodchip path and boardwalks
Trail Markings:	none
Uses:	(pets are not allowed)
Contact:	Braddock Bay Raptor Research
	432 Manitou Beach Road
	Hilton, NY 14468
	or
	NYS DEC Regional Office
	6274 Avon-Lima Road
	Avon, NY 14414
	(716) 226-2466

Trail Directions
· From the parking lot head north across Manitou Beach Road.
· Follow the trail into the pine forest.

145

· At the first junction bear left.
· Three trails lead from the left into the bird-banding field. Please take the center one to visit the blind.
· The trail bends right and takes you over one long and then three short boardwalks.
· Turn left at the trail junction to return to the parking lot.

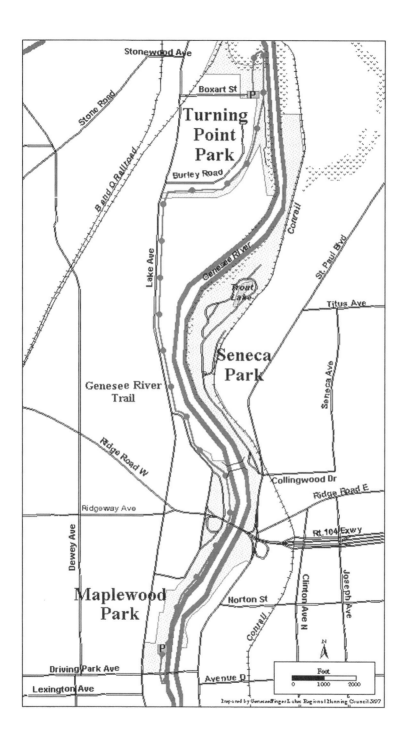

Stonewood Ave

Boxart St   P

Turning Point Park

Burley Road

Stone Road

B and O Railroad

Lake Ave

Genesee River

Trout Lake

Contrail

St. Paul Blvd

Titus Ave

Seneca Park

Seneca Ave

Genesee River Trail

Ridge Road W

Collingwood Dr

Ridge Road E

Ridgeway Ave

Rt. 104 Exwy

Dewey Ave

Clinton Ave N

Joseph Ave

Maplewood Park

Norton St

Contrail

N

P

Driving Park Ave

Avenue D

Feet

Lexington Ave

0   1000   2000

Prepared by Genesee/Finger Lakes Regional Planning Council 3/97

34.
Genesee River Trail

Location:	City of Rochester
Endpoints:	Maplewood Park on Driving Park Avenue or Turning Point Park on Boxart Street (both off Lake Avenue)
Hiking Time:	3.5 hours (round trip)
Length:	7 miles (round trip)
Difficulty:	👣 👣
Surface:	paved path, mowed grass path, dirt path, and sidewalks
Trail Markings:	large Genesee River Trail signs
Uses:	🚶 🎿
Contact:	City of Rochester Department of Parks
	400 Dewey Avenue
	Rochester, NY 14613
	(716) 428-6770

This linear trail is inside the city limits of Rochester and offers good views of the Genesee River from high above to up close. It begins at the south end of Maplewood Park and ends in Turning Point Park. Along the way you'll get a good view of the Genesee River lower falls, cross under the Driving Park and Memorial Bridges, and pass historic King's Landing.

148

History abounds along this area of the gorge. The early settlements of McCrackenville, Carthage, King's Landing, Frankfort, and Castleton are all but memories. Only Charlotte remains a familiar name. With the coming of the Erie Canal, Rochesterville grew. By 1834 the combination of these seven settlements became the city of Rochester.

The parks at either end of this hike are unique public lands. First, manicured Maplewood Park with its rolling hills, perched next to the Genesee River gorge, has 14 acres of rose gardens within it. Next, Turning Point Park covers 100 acres off Lake Avenue at Boxart Street. This forever-wild park, which sits along the west side of the Genesee River, has docks jutting into the river. A visit here will step you back to what Rochester may have looked like 150 years ago. You'll pass old piers where ships tied up. The original docks opened in the 1890s, but only a cement ship comes up the river to deliver its cargo now. This area is the wide-water section of the river where large boats turned around after unloading their cargo. That's how the Turning Point Park got its name. In 1982, a 100-foot long dock was added as a park improvement project.

Trail Directions

· The parking lot for Maplewood Park is off Driving Park Avenue, near the corner of Lake Avenue.

· Begin by walking across Driving Park Avenue toward the YMCA. On the left side of the YMCA parking lot is a yellow metal gate (west side of Driving Park bridge).

· Pass by the gate and head down the paved roadway.

· Part way down, take the stairway on the left and double back along the river. (Straight will take you to Rochester Gas and Electric property.) You're rewarded with a great view of the lower Genesee Falls and the Driving Park Bridge.

· Pass under Driving Park Bridge.

· Just before you head up a flight of stairs, notice the ruins of an old building ahead near the edge of the gorge. This is the foundation for a refreshment stand built in the early 1900s.

· Climb two flights of stairs to return to Maplewood Park. Be sure to read the historic signs about the underground railroad and the Seneca Indian village. Also directly ahead is a popular winter sledding hill. Children of all ages start at the top next to Lake Avenue and slide toward the Maplewood Park parking lot.

· Turn right and follow the fence line as it parallels the river. Genesee River Trail signs will guide you.

· Pass several scenic overlooks with great views of the river's gorge.

· Pass under the Veterans Bridge (Route 104).

· Continue following the fence line. Eventually a right turn would take you to a pedestrian bridge over the river to Seneca Park, but that's a separate hike, so continue straight.

· You'll pass more history: a sign about a palisaded fort of the Indians and a grist stone from Hanford's Mill. Continue along the fence line.

· Pass Eastman Kodak Company's King's Landing Wastewater Treatment plant entrance. Just beyond is a bench with a great view of the river's gorge.

· From the bench on you'll be walking on the sidewalk. Turn right on Lake Avenue and continue on the sidewalk.

· Pass the Kodak research laboratories, Holy Sepulchre Cemetery, and Riverside Cemetery (approximately 1.5 miles on sidewalks.)

· After the cemeteries (just before the Charlotte sign), turn right into Turning Point Park.

· Head downhill on a wide path.

· At the first junction bear right. (Straight will take you directly to the Turning Point Park parking lot, but you'll miss the sights along the river.)

· Further down on your right is an observation deck with a nice waterfall view.

· Continue downhill.

· At river level turn left. (If you wish, you can take a side trip to the right to explore more river front. This short path goes to a dead end.)

· The trail will bend to the left and head uphill.

· Toward the top pass through gray metal gates. Continue on the main path.

· At the top of the hill is the Turning Point Park parking lot and another great view of the river below.

150

Northampton Park

This park is unique because of the active "working" farm within its boundaries. Originally, when the park was dedicated in 1964, it was named Salmon Creek Park. But, Northampton was later selected to honor the area's rich history and the former Township of Northampton.

The park, which straddles the Sweden-Ogden town line, combines a downhill ski slope and rope tow, a model airplane field, Salmon Creek, the Pulver House of the Ogden Historical Society, and Springdale Farm - a demonstration farm with chickens, peacocks, turkeys, horses, cows, goats, bunnies, pigs, lambs, and bulls. It's a great place to explore with children either before or after a hike. The farm is open Monday through Saturday from 10 a.m. to 4 p.m. and Sundays noon to 4 p.m.

The vegetation along the trail is mostly tall bush and young trees. Lots of loop trails along with a picnic pavilion and pond will add to your enjoyment of Northampton Park.

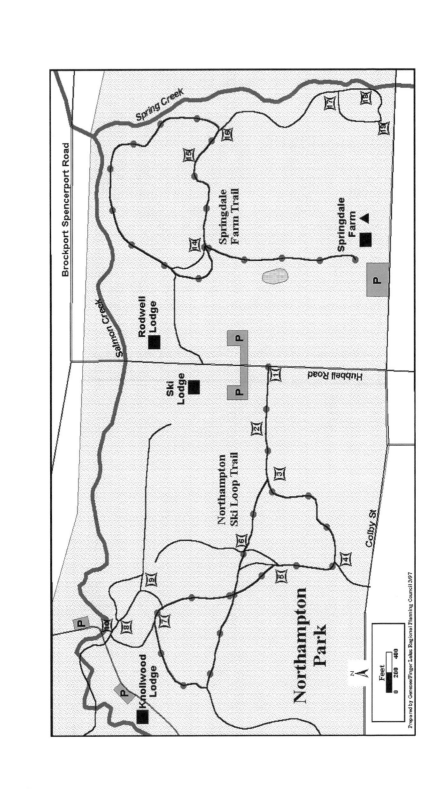

35.
Springdale Farm Trail

Location:	Northampton Park, Colby Street, Ogden
Endpoints:	Springdale Farm parking lot on Colby Street
Hiking Time:	45 minutes
Length:	1.5 miles
Difficulty:	
Surface:	gravel road, dirt path, mowed grass path
Trail Markings:	none
Uses:	
Park Size:	973 acres
Contact:	Monroe County Parks Department
	171 Reservoir Avenue
	Rochester, NY 14620
	(716) 256-4950
	or
	Springdale Farm
	operated by Heritage Christian Home, Inc.
	(716) 352-5320

Trail Directions
· From the parking lot follow the paved path to Springdale Farms barn area.
· The gravel road leads from behind the barns, past a pond (with ducks, geese, and swing seats) to the woods.
· At the "Woodlot Trail" sign the trail turns to dirt and enters the woods.

153

- Bear left at the big red sign and follow the leaf-covered path through beech trees.
- Emerge to a mowed field. Turn left and follow the edge of the field.
- At the bottom of the sled hill (before heading uphill) turn right and cross over the field. Bear right again and follow along the edge of the woods. You're now on the opposite side of the field from where you started.
- Enter the woods. Climb a small hill. A small stream is in a gully to your left.
- Pass through a shrub field. At the junction bear right.
- Emerge into a field. The path follows the edge of a hedgerow then the edge of the woods.
- When you meet a gravel path, turn left and head toward the barns and parking lot.

36.
Northampton Ski Loop Trail

Location:	Northampton Park, Colby Street, Ogden
Endpoints:	parking lot on Hubbell Road near the ski lodge
Hiking Time:	1 hour
Length:	2.0 miles
Difficulty:	👣
Surface:	mowed grass path
Trail Markings:	blue-and-white metal signs on wooden posts at trail junctions
Uses:	🚶 ⛷ 🐎
Park Size:	973 acres
Contact:	Monroe County Parks Department
	171 Reservoir Avenue
	Rochester, NY 14620
	(716) 256-4950

Trail Directions

· Leave the parking lot from the corner farthest from the ski lodge.
· Take the path between fields to a sign "Horse Trailer Parking" and continue straight to junction marker "2."
· Continue straight on the mowed path. Turn left at junction marker "3."

155

- The path goes between woods and a field. At junction marker "4" bear right.
- Notice the old stone fence inside the woods along the right side of the trail.
- At junction marker "5" bear left.
- After the wide mowed area, bear left.
- When the path curves bear right. (Several paths lead off to the left.)
- At junction marker "7" turn right.
- At the wide area turn left.
- Turn left at junction marker "6."
- Bear left at junction marker "3," and you'll return to the parking lot.

City
Neighborhoods

37.
Grove Place Walk

Location:	downtown Rochester
Endpoints:	Metro Center Ramp Garage at corner of Scio Street and East Main Street
Hiking Time:	30 minutes
Length:	1 mile
Difficulty:	
Trail Markings:	none
Uses:	
Information Furnished by:	American Heart Association 2113 Chili Avenue Rochester, NY 14624 (716) 426-4050

Enjoy a downtown stroll past quaint townhouses. Circle Midtown Plaza and Xerox Square on your tour of the best of downtown.

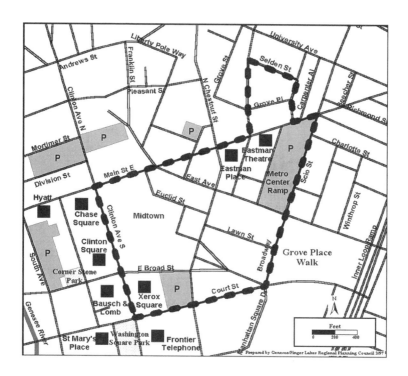

Trail Directions

· Exit the Metro Center Ramp Garage on Scio Street and head north.

· Turn left onto East Main Street and a quick right onto Windsor Street.

· Take a left at Selden Street and another left onto Gibbs Street.

· At East Main Street turn right, walk five blocks, and take a left onto North Clinton Avenue.

· In two blocks turn left onto Court Street.

· In another two blocks turn left onto Broadway.

· Continue straight as Broadway becomes Scio Street, and return to the Metro Center Ramp Garage.

38.

Cornhill District Walk

Location:	downtown Rochester
Endpoints:	Civic Center Garage, Broad Street
Hiking Time:	30 minutes
Length:	1 mile
Difficulty:	
Trail Markings:	none
Uses:	
Information Furnished by:	American Heart Association
	2113 Chili Avenue
	Rochester, NY 14624
	(716) 426-4050

Step back in time as you wander through Corn Hill's neighborhood of restored homes.

Trail Directions
· Exit the Civic Center Garage to Broadway and turn left on Broadway.
· Turn left onto South Plymouth Avenue.
· Cross over Interstate 490 and turn left onto Troup Street.
· Bear right on Fitzhugh Street, go past South Plymouth Avenue.
· Turn right on Edinburgh Street.

160

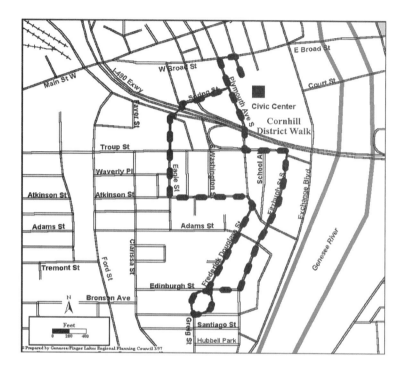

· When you come to Frederick Douglas Street take a left and walk around the circle with the gazebo in the center.
· Continue down Frederick Douglas Street after completing the circle.
· Continue straight ahead through a small park.
· Turn left on South Plymouth Avenue.
· Turn left onto Atkinson Street, then right on onto Eagle Street.
· Continue straight on Livingston Park.
· Head toward the pedestrian bridge and cross over Interstate 490.
· Bear right on Spring Street.
· Turn left on South Plymouth Avenue.
· At Broad Street turn right and return to the Civic Center Garage.

Indoor
Walks

39.
Rochester City Skyway

Location:	downtown Rochester
Endpoints:	Washington Square Garage, corner of South Clinton and Woodbury near GeVa Theater
Hiking Time:	30 minutes
Length:	1 mile
Difficulty:	
Trail Markings:	blue Skyway logo signs
Uses:	(pets are not allowed)
Information Furnished by:	American Heart Association
	2113 Chili Avenue
	Rochester, NY 14624
	(716) 426-4050

OK, we all know there are days when the weather's not quite the best in Rochester. Don't let that stop you. Try the indoor walkway in downtown Rochester. This well-marked network of climate controlled walkways connects a number of major downtown buildings. It gives a bird's-eye view of downtown, its flavor and activities, through large windows. Open 7 a.m. to 7 p.m. Monday through Saturday.

Trail Directions
· Leave Washington Square Garage at level 3 and follow the blue Skyway logos to Midtown Plaza.
· Pass the entrance to Frontier Corp., Xerox Corp., and Bausch & Lomb Inc.
· Travel twice around the second level at Midtown.
· Exit toward Lincoln Tower, pass through the Rochester Riverside Convention Center, and on to the Sheraton Four Points Hotel (formerly the Holiday Inn.)
· Turn around and retrace your steps to Washington Square Garage.

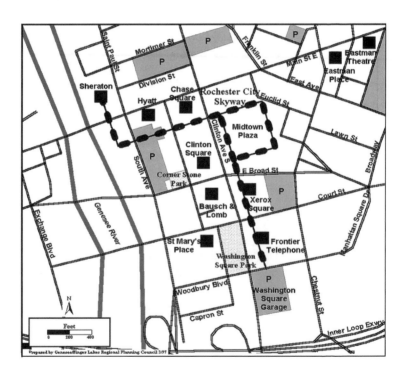

40.
Mall and School Walks

Information provided by The American Heart Association

This may be the farthest thing from getting close to nature, but with Rochester's weather, it is a nice alternative. You can maintain your healthy activity even in the worst of weather and window shop too! For further information contact the American Heart Association. Ask for details of the "Ongoing Walks Programs" along with any sponsored walks in the future.

Monroe County: (716) 426-4050

Ontario and Wayne Counties: (716) 394-1240

Malls

Location Days Available	Times Available
Eastview Mall Daily	8 a.m. to 8:30 a.m.
Greece Ridge Center Daily	8 a.m. to 10 p.m.
Irondequoit Mall Daily	8 a.m. to 10 p.m.
Marketplace Mall Monday through Saturday	6 a.m. to 10 p.m.
Perinton Square Mall Monday through Friday Saturday	7 a.m. to 9 p.m. 7 a.m. to 6 p.m.

165

School Walks

Schools

Location
Days Available   **Times Available**

Brighton High School
1150 Winton Road South
    Monday through Thursday   6:30 p.m. to 9:30 p.m.

Churchville
Fairbanks Elementary School
175 Fairbanks Road
    Monday through Friday   4 p.m. to 8 p.m.

Fairport
Northside - Dudley School
181-211 Hamilton Road
    Monday through Friday   6:45 a.m. to 8 a.m.
        5:30 p.m. to 8:30 p.m.

Gates/Chili High School
910 Wegman Road
cafeteria entrance
    Monday through Thursday   5 p.m. to 8:30 p.m.

Palmyra/Macedon School
Hyde Parkway
    Monday through Friday   6:15 a.m. to 7:15 a.m.
        4 p.m. to 6 p.m.

Penfield
Cobbles Elementary School
Gebhardt Road
    Monday through Friday   6:30 a.m. to 8:30 a.m.
        4 p.m. to 10 p.m.

🐾 👣 School Walks

Location
    Days Available   **Times Available**

Pittsford Middle School
Barker Road
    Monday through Friday   4 p.m. to 8:30 p.m.

Rush Henrietta
Fyle Elementary
133 Vollmer Parkway
    Tuesday through Thursday   3 p.m. to 9 p.m.

Rush Henrietta
Leary Elementary
5509 E. Henrietta Road
    Monday, Wednesday, and Thursday   3 p.m. to 9 p.m.

Rush Henrietta
Crane Elementary
85 Shell Edge Drive
    Tuesday through Thursday   4:30 p.m. to 9 p.m.

Rush Henrietta
Sherman School
50 Authors Avenue
    Monday, Wednesday, and Friday   3 p.m. to 9 p.m.

Rush Henrietta
Winslow School
755 Pinacle Road
    Tuesday, Wednesday, and Thursday   4 p.m. to 9 p.m.

Rush Henrietta
Burger Middle School
639 Erie Station Road
    Monday through Friday   6 p.m. to 9 p.m.

Location
  Days Available   **Times Available**

Rush Henrietta
Roth Middle School
4000 East Henrietta Road
  Monday through Friday   6 p.m. to 9 p.m.

Rush Henrietta
Senior High School
1799 Lehigh Station Road
  Monday through Friday   6 p.m. to 9 p.m.

Spencerport
Townline Road School
399 Ogden-Parma Townline Road
  Monday through Friday   4 p.m. to 7 p.m.

Webster High School
875 Ridge Road
  Monday through Thursday   4 p.m. to 9 p.m.

Reference List

Adirondack Mountain Club
Genesee Valley Chapter
(716) 987-1717

American Heart Association
Genesee Valley Region
2113 Chili Avenue
Rochester, NY 14624
(716) 426-4050

Braddock Bay Raptor Research
432 Manitou Beach Road
Hilton, NY 14468

Crescent Trail Association
P.O. Box 1354
Fairport, NY 14450

Eastern Mountain Sports (EMS)
Irondequoit Mall
(716) 266-5460
Marketplace Mall
(716) 272-0090

Friends of the Genesee Valley Greenway, Inc.
16 Chapel Street
Mount Morris, NY 14510
(716) 658-2569

Ganondagan State Historic Site
P.O. Box 239
1488 Victor-Holcomb Road
Victor, NY 14564-0239
(716) 924-5848

Reference List

Grassroots Shoe Store
1225 Jefferson Road
Rochester, NY 14623
(716) 475-1322

Hansen Nature Center
1585 Calkins Road
P.O. Box 999
Henrietta, NY 14467-0999
(716) 359-7044

Helmer Nature Center
154 Pinegrove Avenue
Rochester, NY 14617
(716) 336-3035

Letchworth State Park Interpretive Program
1 Letchworth State Park
Castile, NY 14427
(716) 493-3625

Monroe County Parks Department
171 Reservoir Avenue
Rochester, NY 14620
(716) 256-4950

Monroe County Public Library
Rundel Memorial Building
Local History Section
115 South Avenue
Rochester, NY 14604
(716) 428-7300

NYS DEC Regional Office
6274 Avon-Lima Road
Avon, NY 14414
(716) 226-2466

Pack, Paddle, Ski, Corp.
Box 82
South Lima, NY 14558
(716) 346-5597

Pittsford Parks Department
35 Lincoln Avenue
Pittsford, NY 14534
(716) 248-6280

Pittsford Trails Coalition
Pittsford Parks
35 Lincoln Avenue
Pittsford, NY 14534
(716) 248-6280

Rochester Birding Association
(716) 425-4630

Rochester Orienteering Club
(716) 367-5650

Snow Country
Pittsford Plaza
Pittsford, NY 14618
(716) 586-6460

Snow Country
Parkway Plaza
Canandaigua, NY 14424
(716) 398-2300

Springdale Farm
operated by Heritage Christian Home, Inc.
(716) 352-5320

Tent City
47 Parkway
Rochester, NY 14608
(716) 458-0170

Tent City
950 Ridge Road
Webster, NY 14580
(716) 787-2255

The Nature Conservancy
315 Alexander Street
Rochester, NY 14604
(716) 546-8030

Town of Penfield
3100 Atlantic Avenue
Penfield, NY 14526
(716) 377-8674

Town of Victor
85 East Main Street
Victor, NY 14564
(716) 924-7141

Victor Hiking Trails, Inc.
85 East Main Street
Victor, NY 14564

Webster Parks, Recreation and Community Services
1000 Ridge Road
Webster, NY 14580
(716) 872-2911

Web Sites

Rochester is an active hiking community. And, once involved in local hiking, you may be bitten by the bug and want to travel further afield to the southern tier, the Adirondack Mountains, or beyond. Information abounds on the Internet for both local and non-local hiking opportunities.

Some of the hiking clubs such as Crescent Trails and Victor Hiking Trails offer guided hikes and publish their schedules on their Internet pages.

Here are a few Web sites worth checking out:

Adirondack Mountain Club (Genesee Valley Chapter)
www.frontiernet.net/~dbaird/gvc.htm

Crescent Trail Association
www.ggw.org/freenet/c/ctha/index.html

Finger Lakes Trail
www.fingerlakes.net/trailsystem/

Friends of the Finger Lakes
www.fingerlakes.com/

Genesee Valley Greenway
www.netacc.net/~fogvg

Great Outdoor Recreation Page
www.gorp.com/

Hikes in Ontario County
www.ontariony.com/

Hiking with Canines

http//snapple.cs.washington.edu/canine/backpacking

www.coyotecom.com/dogcamp.html

www.allpets.com/alldogs/alldogs.html

New York State Hiking Trails

www.servtech.com/public/rbs/ny/

Orienteering

www.servtech.com/public/egmayer/orient.htm

Rail-Trail Resource Center

www.rail-trail.org/fredwert/

Rochester Online

www.RochesterNY.com

Rochester Orienteering Club

www.servtech.com/public/egmayer/roc.htm

Rochester Outdoors

www.servtech.com/public/maxlent/outdoor.htm

Rochester Bicycling Club

www.win.net/~rbcbbs

Victor Hiking Trails Inc.

www.ggw.org/freenet/v/vht

 **Trails By Length**

⚜ 🐾 Trails By Length

Combine Trails For A Longer Hike

Trail Of Peace + Earth Is Our Mother Trail =	2.4 miles
Irondequoit Creek Trail + Fish Hatchery Trail =	3.0 miles
Hardwood Swamp Trail + Field Loop =	3.5 miles
Springdale Farm Trail + Northampton Ski Loop Trail =	3.5 miles
Horizon Hill Section + McCoord Woods Section =	4.6 miles
Quaker Pond Trail + Devil's Bathtub Trail =	5.4 miles
Eastern Ski Trail + Pine Forrest Loop =	7.4 miles

Trails By Difficulty

One Boot

Trails By Difficulty

Two Boots

Three Boots

Four Boots

Loop vs. Linear Trails

Linear Trails

Loop Trails

Loop Trails

Educational Trails

Historical Trails

Word Index

182

183

185

Word Index

About The Authors

Rich and Sue Freeman not only know western New York well, as natives of Webster and Fairport, but have an intimate sense for trails, developed on their 2,000-mile thru-hike of the Appalachian Trail. This intense experience heightened their affinity for nature. Rich says "If something is bothering you, or you're looking for answers, go for a walk in the woods. Things become clearer, and more focused. Life's distractions are not there, only the essentials of nature." Sue adds, "Rochester has a wealth of diverse trails to explore and lend clarity to anyone's life."

For the past five years Rich and Sue have been active, founding members of Victor Hiking Trails, helping to establish some of the trails listed in this book. Both were professionals working for large corporations - Sue as a director of marketing and Rich as a manager of customer service. After the Appalachian Trail experience, they have refocused their life priorities and are currently reviewing self-employment business opportunities and enjoying the search for new adventures and trails to hike.

Yes, I'd like my very own copy of

*Family Walks
in the
Rochester Area*

Enclosed is $16.95 plus $3 for shipping, handling, and tax. Total $19.95 per book.

\# Copies: _____

Your Name: _____

Address: _____

City: _____

State: _____ Zip: _____

Make check payable and mail to:
Footprint Press
P.O. Box 645-R
Fishers, NY 14453

Watch for book # 2

Take A Hike!
Family Walks **South**
Of Rochester